Jeel Shah

The Clockworks of Wall Street

To my parents, Nitin and Rita Shah
To my brother, Neel
To Hammad Khan, my mentor
To my Friends
To my Family
And to *you*

Contents

Acknowledgements

No book can be made by one person alone. Even though the author is the one that writes that book, that is only half or even quarter of the story. There are lots of people that I would like to thank even for the little pointers that they provided but here are the few that made most if not all of it happen.

I would like to thank my mentor, Hammad Khan, for providing information about the topic and reviewing the book. I would like to thank Jessica Lai whom I accidentaly met while at a conference and was fortunate enough to see her beautiful work and had the courage to ask her to design the book cover. Thank you Jessica, the cover is much more than I expected. I would also like to thank Nikunj Varshney for taking the time to convert Jessica's book into a digital version. I would also like to thank my uncle Harit Shah for providing editing services and doing what he does best, solving problems.

In addition, I would like to thank my friend, Rohail Sultan who, in the nick of time, came to the rescue and re-edited the book.

Introduction

I was always fascinated with the things around me, wondering why they existed and how they functioned. I was very curious as a child, which often led me into trouble but I cannot say that I regret being curious.

I remember a particular instance, when I was maybe four or five and still living in India, the country where I was born, when I proved to myself that time or growth existed in some sense. Like every boy, I owned a toy gun that shot foam bullets and I recall that my father had bought it for me when I was maybe three or something, I can't say for sure. Anyway, the gun had been lost for some time, maybe a year, until I found it laying underneath my bed.

I recall, that I was very astonished at the size of the gun, remembering that when I got it, it was very big and it could hardly fit in the palm of my hand but now, I could hold it. It did not make much sense to me but I reasoned as much as any four year old could. I thought to myself that either this gun got smaller or I got bigger. For some reason, I disregarded the idea that the gun could get smaller, I was probably thinking that it was not living and therefore, could not decrease in size. This meant, that I had grown bigger. "Wow" I thought to myself, I have grown bigger.

Exactly what "bigger" meant, I did not know but the fact that the gun could now fit into the palm of my hand, made me feel good. What caused to get bigger? This, among other questions were at the top of my list that I wanted to have answered. Of course, I never had the question *officially* answered but I was suffice with the fact I had figured out that things were getting smaller as I was growing bigger. "It was all about perspective", I thought. My fascination continued as I grew older and learned new and more interesting things. I continued to question the various things I learned on a daily basis, something I recommend that every do and furthermore, continued to learn while I questioned.

Along came high school, which quite frankly was not too long ago when my interest in finance grew to more than occasionally watching the news. I was always interested to know what the guys on T.V were talking about when used "big" words and talked about the economy like it was an organism from a different planet, which it kind of is. So, like any person, I began to learn about stocks and bonds because *that's all there is to finance* - stock and bonds. I learned what I could and laid my finance curiosity to rest. When I started to get back into finance and conduct research for this book, I was extremely shocked that nowhere in my previous learning had I come across things such as options or hedge funds or specialists which by the way are three *very* different things. It was almost as if I had been cheated and I was furious. I realized that the resources I used to learn never pointed me to other concepts. The vision was narrow due to my learning and may not have widened if I had not researched for this book. It was then that I decided that if I should write a book about anything, it should give the reader the opportunity to explore and tell them about the possibilities that exist. In all fairness, however, some of the concepts, had I been introduced to them then, would have confused the heck out of me but it would have still been nice if I known they existed.

Atlanta - More Like on the Way There

I really did not want to go to Atlanta but I am really glad that I did because that flight would change everything.

In my hand was Michael Gazzaniga's *Human*, which by the way is a fantastic read for anyone who is interested in neuroscience. Beside me was a gentleman who was also reading another great book, *Thinking, Fast and Slow* but I was not aware of its magnificence at the time. The gentleman, leaned over and asked "Can I see that?" I thought, sure why not?

T−10 seconds later, we started a conversation that lasted the entire flight to Atlanta and by the end of it I had found my mentor, Hammad Khan, who is one of the persons to which this book is dedicated.

The idea for the novel was not given to me then but through e-mail conversation, Hammad suggested to me that I write a book that I wished I had. By the way, the motivation for writing this book was to reduce the amount of sleep I had and let me tell you that I have been successful at that. As a matter of fact, Hammad suggested to me that I either learned Mandarin, learn how to play the piano or write a book, two of which I already tried and failed (Mandarin and the piano). I always wanted to write a book of some sort. As a matter of fact, I had tried a couple of times before but it never seemed to work out but now I had the guidance of my mentor, a purpose and a goal.

The Process

The first thing I did was to subscribe to various finance blogs and newspapers. I wanted to know everything that happened in the finance world even if I did not understand a word of it. It was important to get into the culture of finance and furthermore, understand the possibilities that could arise. I need to build a foundation for myself to stand on. A foundation, I realized, was extremely important to learning because if I wanted to build my finance acumen then I had to make sure I did not have gaps. As I learned more about finance, It dawned on me that finance was exactly the opposite of what I thought it might be and quite frankly, it was nothing short of wonder.

It is commonly thought that finance is a boring subject that requires no imagination and creativity whatsoever. That could not be more far more the truth. I could argue that finance requires the same amount of imagination and creativity as any other field in the world, the only difference is the tools and the motive. On one hand, you have a "quant" who implements various algorithms to exploit the markets and on another hand, you have a physicist who implements the same concepts to figure out the mysteries of the universe however as Dali said in Woody Allen's *Midnight in Paris* "Is there a difference? In the beauty?" Superficially, yes, there is a difference but upon closer inspection, one realizes that there isn't. The two, in some ways, are linked and when the logic or the cleverness is shown, the beauty of the two remains the same.

Not only was it important to be surrounded by finance related news but it was also important to gain the vernacular that was used. To achieve this, I subscribed to blogs, something I recommend that everyone do. By subscribing to these blogs, I was able to gain blunt information, without the excessive flair and get it from people who worked in the industry and not from people who reported on it.

This process continued, until I had found and gathered the necessary information for this book. If there is anything you are going to take from this book, then it should be to stay curious and keep open mind. Without both of those things, I would have never been able to write this book.

The (Real) Purpose

Aside from the fact that I initially decided to write this book because I wanted to sleep less, I really wanted people to read the book and gain a thorough understanding of finance and not just make opinions based on what they heard from individuals.

It was very evident to me that things that were related to finance were largely misunderstood by my friends and family. Some of them threw around terms they did not understand completely. This only caused them to make uninformed opinions about the world around them. In order for us to grow and learn, we must have people around us that are informed about the things that they talk about. Therefore, it is the purpose of this book to take people who hardly understand finance or better yet, people who *think* they know and understand (but in reality they do not) and have them understand the various facets of the field.

That way, everyone will be able to understand and learn properly about the markets and finance. Otherwise, we are all fated to grow slowly and have uninformed decisions passed around the table.

What You Are Going to Learn And Structure

As you may have already figured out, this book is not for individuals that are already well versed in finance-speak. This book is for individuals who have little knowledge and understanding of the markets.

The book starts out with the basics such as assets and liabilities and then aims to move into more advanced topics. The primary idea is to help build a foundation that will allow your curiosity to grow.

Without a strong foundation any field it is difficult to advance in it. For example, it is difficult to do Algebra when your fundamental understanding of integers is incorrect. This is the same for finance. Even though finance is not particularly cumulative, it is a field where you are required to infer – a lot.

Therefore, it is important that whatever you learn is understood well and is reliable. Throughout the book, you will notice the lack of Math or very little Math and that is for good reason. Even though Mathematics makes ideas and concepts easier to convey, I believe that anything can be done through good examples and that will be the case.

Book Layout

The layout of the book is such that the simple ideas come first and then more complex ideas are introduced later. However obvious this may seem, I have seen numerous books that talk about ideas that have yet to fully explain.

However, you will notice that I give examples that are going to be explained later in the book and that is for good reason. Just being hinted about the idea that something like the example exists can make all the difference. I do not want you to start to with a narrow playing field and then expand that playing field. I would like you to start with a large spectrum and fill in spots as you go along. To help you with this, the books contains various definitions right after a concept is introduced.

> An **asset** is something you own... Assets: items of ownership convertible into cash

Notice, how assets is bolded, which shows the significance and right afterwards is the definition. That will be the theme when new words are introduced. The definition that is provided will be simple and closely related to casual discussion to avoid confusion. Practically, this cannot be done always but important words or words of note will be bolded to indicate that the word should be remembered to paid attention to.

Who's Julian?

I have learned through various resources and personal experience that using a story to remember things is extremely useful. Therefore, at the beginning of each chapter and through some of them, you will encounter a character named "Julian."

At the beginning of every chapter, Julian will discover [the title of the chapter] and what he could do with the information that he has attained. He will ask lots of questions which is a sign that you should also be asking those questions. With him is his mentor, George who will guide him and teach him things he does not understand.

The entire premise of the narrative at the beginning of each chapter is to give you a scope of what's to come and give you a general feel and set a mood for the chapter.

Final Thoughts

Before, you jump into the actual book, I just wanted to give you a few tips that my mentor gave to me when I was learning about the markets.

Firstly, keep an open mind. This really goes for anything but more than most things, it goes for the markets. If don't give an open mind, you will never know what is lurking around corner and therefore, will never explore. Be sure to embrace all ideas and their avenues.

Secondly, read, read and read. I cannot stress this enough. If you don't take anything out of this book, at least take the part about reading. To be on top of the game, you have to know what's happening where and its importance. Don't limit yourself to just one newspaper, diversify your portfolio to five newspapers or maybe even ten newspapers! You may be asking yourself "Why is he getting me to read the business section of a newspaper, when I don't know much?" Well, here is the reason why. Even though you may not know the terms that are used, you will at least have been introduced to them. This way, new words/concepts won't be such a surprise to you because you have already seen them.

Well, that's it from me. I really hope that you enjoy the book and learn as much I intended you to learn and more. Hopefully, by the end you will be reading the business section as easily as you cut butter in the morning for your bread.

Good luck!

Chapter 1

Asset Class

Julian is a boy that is not of age but is curious like you and I and likes to explore the world around him. He has been learning about the markets and has started from the basics to build his foundations.

He visits a site that shows him various financials securities, something he does not know in detail yet. "There are so many of them" he wonders, "how does anyone keep track of these?"

He begins to think of the various implications that could come about when dealing with these many securities and instruments. He thinks, whoever is dealing with these securities has to come up with a way to manage them and understand characteristics about them. Of course, this is a tedious job but people must do it anyway. After a half hour of trying to figure out how all of these securities are managed, he's stumped.

He thinks "This doesn't make any sense. Why in the world does everyone have to learn about so many securities separately? Is there not a way for someone to group these securities by various characteristics into classes? Would that not be easier?" This is a fair question that Julian has posed and now we will deal with.

1.1   Starting Off - the Basics

Julian has offered a logical and straightforward idea. Why not just group these securities, that have similar characteristics, into various categories? Julian right indeed and saved himself some work since they already exist. However, instead of referring to them as categories, we'll refer to them as "classes" because that is the traditional way and we'll attach the word "asset" in front of it to dictate the type of class.

Some of you may already know what an "asset" is but it doesn't hurt to review the concept. An **asset** is something that *you* own.

> Assets: items of ownership convertible into cash. `Investopedia.com`

We may get a little philosophical here but it is important for you to understand exactly what it means to own something. There is misconception that some people when they believe they own their house even when they have a mortgage on it. That's not true at all. The house is technically not yours until you have paid for it and obviously a mortgage does not mean you have paid for it. To reiterate, assets are things that you own and not things that you have loan on. Here are a few such examples:

- Cash

- Car

- *Your* paid house

- Computer

- Goodwill

A Category Within A Category?

Assets are divided into two categories tangible and intangible. Tangible assets are assets that are physical and assets that can be held and intangible assets are assets that cannot be held or are not physical. Goodwill, for example, is categorized as an intangible asset because it is not physical or cannot be held but it still has some monetary value. Other examples of intangible assets may be trademarks or copyrights.

Assets are only half of the story. Have you ever had a conversation where the person did not speak of its counterpart, the liability? I doubt it. Even though the chapter is about asset classes, it is important to understand the concept of a liability. A **liability** can be seen as something that is owed.

> Liability: moneys owed; debts or pecuniary obligations. Investopedia.com

Here are a few examples of what a liability could be:

- Any loan e.g. Bank loan

- Salaries/Wages

1.2 Asset Classes, Actually This Time

Now that we have gotten that out of the way, we can finally move onto the actual topic of discussion and that is asset classes.

Julian's idea of what an asset class ought to be is perfectly correct. It is simple categorization of assets that share similar characteristics. Having the ability to have the information about an asset class instantly makes you more knowledgeable than you were and gives you the ability to make inferences extremely quickly. For example, understanding the nature of an asset class can instantly tell you about the nature of its constituents, since all the assets in the asset class share similar characteristics.

The breakdown of asset classes will work as such: first the definition then examples that include the most common constituents in the asset class and common characteristics such as risk. By breaking them down in this fashion, you will gain a deeper understanding of the class and its components. Furthermore, the lesson will be in a narrative style like the first you encountered at the beginning of the chapter. Narratives are a wonderful way to understand concepts and link them together. Hopefully, the narrative does what it has been intended to do. Let's begin!

Julian is Back and He's Brought the "Commodity Asset Class"

As you may know, Julian is a curious character and he enjoys learning through experience more than through plain textbook. According to his mentor, one of the most important asset classes is the **commodity** asset class and one of the best places to learn about commodities is at the commodities market where commodities are bought and sold as futures. Julian doesn't know what futures are but they are not important at the moment, all Julian wants to do is to figure out "what in the world are commodities?"

With his nifty new suit, a shiny blue tie and polished black shoes, he is off to the Chicago Futures Exchange. Upon arrival, he is greeted by his mentor who shows him around. He explains to Julian that commodities are commonly referred to as goods.

> Commodity: A good or service but more commonly a good

Julian's mentor George provides him with a few examples that may help him understand the types of commodities there can be and begins to list a few.

- Sugar

- Coffee beans

- Iron ore

- Coal

- Gas

- Gold

"Now, Julian, commodities are separated into two main factions: soft commodities and hard commodities. Soft commodities are commodities that are grown such as wheat or coffee beans and hard commodities are commodities that are extracted from the ground such as coal or oil."

Julian has somewhat of curious yet puzzled look on his face. He wonders if there can be categories within categories. Hesitantly, Julian asks "George, can we have categories within categories? For example, if I wanted to separate all of the hard commodities such as oil, coal and natural gas into their own category, would that be possible?" George replies swiftly "Of course you can! As a matter of fact, there does exist a category where the energy commodities are separated and dealt with on their own."

Julian is thrilled that he knows what commodities are and their classifications. Of course, one wonders about the risks associated with commodities. One of the ways instruments are classified is through their risk and anything that has a reward must have a risk.

All asset classes carry some sort of risk, some classes are more risky than others for one reason or another. There are no asset classes that have little risk and more reward in comparison to an asset class that has a lot of risk and a lot of reward. For example, if I have an instrument that is very safe, then I can assume the payout will be lower than an instrument that is much more risky. The general rule of thumb is if the risk is high so will be reward and if the risk is low then so will the reward. In a bastardized sense, risk is proportional to reward.

Outside the exchange, the weather is rainy and as the raindrops fall on Julian's head, he begins to think about the risks that are associated with the commodity asset class. Nearby, is "Shelby's" a homely diner, where George and Julian sometimes go for lunch. They enter the diner, as the thunder rolls and the lightning surges through the clouds. They brush off their coats of the cold and call for a menu. The T.V. is on, as it is in most diners and Julian notices that a country is refusing to budge on its oil policy. OilLand, is the largest producer of oil in the world and recently they have decided to stop exporting oil to other nations in the world. Julian wonders if this has anything to do with the wonky prices of oil futures on the Chicago Exchange.

"Hey George, did you hear? OilLand has decided to stop the export of Oil to other nations. Is this the reason why oil futures have such wonky prices?"

"Well, Commodities carry something called 'geopolitical risk'. It may sound like a large term but the concept is fairly simple to understand. Suppose, we have a country, such as OilLand whose oil production and distribution is controlled. Now understand, Julian, oil is a hot commodity and people need it. So they are willing to pay the necessary price. If the supply of oil is low then the demand for it will be high and so will the price. Therefore, by constricting the flow of the oil from the country, the price of oil is going up. But you have to know that the example I have provided is in a perfect world. This is assuming that OilLand is one of the only producers of oil and controls a lot of the market and that is not the case in the real world."

An Explanation

As George said, the example provided is set in a perfect world or in a world where one country controls a lot of oil exports. Geopolitical risk is common on the commodities market because commodities are actual goods that need to be produced or grown somewhere. If that is restricted then, logically, so will the flow of those goods from one country to another.

What's important to understand is that geopolitical risk is not inherently good or bad. It merely depends on the perspective you are taking. If you are a short seller (we'll be discussing short selling in later chapters) then you want the price of the commodity to go down rather then up or vice versa, if you are betting that the price of oil will increase then geopolitical risk will be, in some sense, bad for you. Therefore, assessing geopolitical risk is really dependant on the perspective of the buyer/seller.

Furthermore, geopolitical doesn't always mean that a country is freeing its resources/distribution. It could also mean that a country might be restricting its resources/distribution. Suppose, we have a country who has been exporting oil since its inception but now has decided to nationalize the oil, which will restrict foreign investment or not allow foreign companies from starting their own establishments there. Therefore, the trader has to also recognize the other side of geopolitical risk.

I have developed a few questions to ask yourself when trying to assess the risk of commodities. These questions won't necessarily assess risk for you but they will help your thought process. One of the most important things to do when assessing risks is to see the whole picture. Therefore, the primary purpose of these questions is to give you the big picture. Then from the macro you can move to micro. It goes without saying that you need to develop your own intuitive feeling for risk but a little help doesn't hurt.

- Is the country politically unstable from your perspective?

- Are you benefiting from instability?

- Is this instability for the better or the worse?

Speculation

Investors are always looking for ways to make lots of money and fast. They have several methods at their disposal and the most common one is **speculation**. To put simply speculation is the process of making money in the short term by predicting the fluctuations in price and then acting on them. Here is the formal definition.

> Speculation: the practice of making money through risky investments, in the "hopes" that investment will gain substantially over a short amount of time.

Suppose Julian, our novice investor wants to make money quick and he has some gut feeling. Julian picks a stock after long analysis and waits for a very short amount of time. What Julian aims to do is to *speculate*. He wants the price of his stock to move up very quickly, just for a few moments so he can make his profit. The higher the jump, the more money Julian can make. Luckily, Julian's hunch pays off and he is successful in his bet. Just like

Julian there are thousands of other traders hoping to do the same.

The primary problem with speculation is that it may get out of hand. For instance, a speculator may dump $1 000 into a commodity future and hope that within a short amount of time the price of that future goes up, so he/she can sell it and make a healthy profit. Now imagine, thousands of these speculators doing the same thing, either betting with the future or against it. Suppose more than half these speculators are wrong then what will be the consequence? The price of that future will become more volatile or to put simply, the price of the future will fluctuate more and in a shorter amount of time. By increasing the risk associated with it and increasing the chances you will lose money when trading the future.

"So you see Julian? Commodities are an important asset class to take notice of. They provide an alternate investment with decent risk and reward. They carry a few inherent risks that we have discussed and are fairly simple to understand. All you have to remember is that there are two types of commodities: hard and soft and that two types of risks primarily effect commodities, namely geopolitical risk and speculation."

"I can't believe commodities were this easy to understand. But I have another question for you George, I have heard of Stocks and private equity. Surely these must also be categorized into another asset class? If I am not mistaken, these have different risks and rewards right?"

Equity Asset Class

The equity asset class is one of the most known asset classes out there. Everyone knows about its constituents as they are extremely popular. Before Julian asks anymore questions we need to quickly get some things out of the way. Firstly, what is **equity**? Equity is the direct ownership of an asset.

> Equity: The direct ownership of an asset after all liabilities, in relation to the asset, have been paid.

The definition is somewhat confusing because what does it mean to have direct ownership of an asset? Isn't owning a commodity future (a future is like a contract) having direct ownership? A futures contract is a contract that promises to buy or sell at a given date in the future, the owner does own what he is to buy or sell. For example, if I have a wheat future that says "I will give you 100 bushels of wheat if the price rises above 100/bushel" then you have indirect ownership of the 100 bushels of wheat. In essence you have a contract that says that if condition A is fulfilled then fulfil condition B otherwise fulfil condition C which is generally nothing. Furthermore, it is not necessary for you to own something to sell it. This may sound a little convoluted but you will later find that it is quite logical.

Julian and his mentor, take a trip to the world famous New York Stock Exchange (NYSE). This is the place where stocks, among other things are bought and sold. When people speak of the "markets" they are generally referring to an exchange such as the NYSE. Julian does not quite understand what a stock is and pokes at his mentor for some guidance. George explains that a stock is an equity investment because it gives the owner of the stock (a bundle of shares) a portion of the company. "Suppose" says George "that company ABC is selling all of its 100 shares. You manage to buy 51 of those shares and since you own 51 shares of 100, you own 51% of the company. Does that make sense?" Julian nods. This is not necessarily true, as you will find out in Chapter 3.

The main idea to take away from this example is to understand how owning shares is an equity investment. Shares are portions of companies and since you are buying those shares, you directly own a portion of the company. Therefore, making it an equity investment.

There are many types of equities that exist therefore, there is a category within a category. The first category we will deal with is a **listed equity** and it only has one constituent.

> Listed Equity: A share of a public company that can be found on a Stock Exchange.

The definition could not be simpler! A listed equity is basically a stock that could be found on an exchange. There are also equities that are not on any particular stock exchange and these are known as **private equities**. The definition is simplified but it maintains the gist.

> Private Equity: The equity of a company that is not found on a Stock Exchange.

Julian is sitting in his favourite seat at his favourite diner, when he comes up with a brilliant idea, an idea that may just revolutionize the world. He thinks to himself "What if, I can create a machine that will do all my chores?" Let's not forget, Julian is still a student. "Yes!" Says Julian "That's exactly what I'll do and I'll name it the Chorinator. But where am I to get the funds? How can I start making my 'Chorinator' if I don't have the means?"

Julian is in a deep conundrum, he wants to invent something but he doesn't have the means to do so. The first thing that comes to mind is to ask for a loan from a bank. But banks don't invest in ideas that may win or lose, they only want to invest in certainties and Julian's idea is no certainty! Julian has only one option and that is to find a private equity investor. A private equity investor will analyse Julian's idea and determine the feasibility from his/her perspective and determine if he/she is to profit from such an idea.

A private equity investor named Jim seems to be interested in Julian's idea. He analyses the designs and sees that profit can be made. Jim decides to invest in Julian's idea and has agreed to provide Julian with the $500 000 for 40% of the company. Julian, with his new found investment, gets cracking on the "Chorinator".

Julian has successfully gained the funds necessary for him to build his idea but what he lost? Let's analyse the deal, which Jim has made. Jim has given Julian $500 000 for 40% of company. Therefore, Jim owns 40% of Julian's company and furthermore, has 40% say in what Julian does. By owning 40% of the company, Jim can incur 40% of the total losses or he can gain 40% of the total profits. By having equity in the company, Jim is now a part of it and where the company goes, up or down, Jim goes along for the ride.

Many start-ups are funded in the same way Julian's idea was funded by Jim but that is not the only type of private equity investment.

More often then not, you will encounter private equity firms whose purpose is to buy insolvent (enterprises that cannot pay off their debts) companies and then turn them around in order to make a profit. The basic process for any private equity firm is to reduce inefficiencies/redundancies and sell assets to make the company profitable again.

Suppose, we have a private equity firm named MoneyMakers Capital. Their primary purpose, like we said, is to buy an insolvent company, turn it around and then sell it.

ABC Inc. is a company that has been on the market for over two decades. They specialize in transporting goods from one place to another through shipping and air. The recent change in management has caused the company to lose profitability. If there isn't change, the company will soon go bankrupt.

MoneyMakers has had an eye on ABC for quite a while and have noticed the same thing ABC has. From MoneyMakers' perspective, this is a perfect opportunity for them to buy the company and to try and make a profit. They buy the company for $500mn and begin the process of making the company profitable again. They first try to identify the inefficiencies that exist in the workplace and begin to remove them. This could mean reducing staff, increasing the work hours, reducing pay etc. All

MoneyMakers wants to do is to make the company profitable again, so they can sell it again to make a profit. Over the next two years, the company becomes profitable again and MoneyMakers manages to resell ABC for a $1bn, pocketing 500mn$ as profit.

It's not necessary for MoneyMakers Capital to resell the company, they can keep the company and gain the profits the company makes. Therefore, MoneyMakers has two options: to sell the company whole or to gain the possible profits the company can make.

Private equity risks are more intuitive then most people would think. The premise of any private equity firm or investor is either to invest in an insolvent company, in hopes of turning it around or to invest in an idea, which may profit in the future. The central problem is that private equity investors can't see the future, no one can. If an investment sours in the future, the only thing they can do is insure against it. The best possible route a private equity investor/firm can take is to deeply analyse a company's financials and determine whether or not they can turn the company profitable. Therefore, one of the only risks to private equity investment is your own judgement.

"So you see Julian? The equity asset class has a class of its own. It gives the investor the opportunity to be a part of something big. The investor can either invest in listed equities such as stocks, they can fund a project or turn a company into profit through private equity. But, you know, there is a much safer class you can opt for if you aren't interested in the equity asset class." Says George

"And what would that be?"
"The Fixed Interest Asset class"

The Fixed Interest Asset Class

The Fixed Interest asset class is one of the easiest asset classes to understand. The etymology of the words "Fixed Interest" will easily help us understand what the class entails.

The name "Fixed Interest" comes from the nature of the constituents in the class. The class contains instruments such as government bonds or corporate bonds that yield returns depending on the interest they carry and the time they carry it for. Furthermore, Fixed Interest securities are extremely predictable because they indicate exactly how much they will pay out in x years.

To understand the Fixed Interest asset class, one must understand bonds. Since, the next chapter deals with Stocks and Bonds, I won't be diving into the topic too much. I want you to get a basic feel for what a bond is so you can understand the Fixed Interest asset class.

A bond is a government/corporate issued IOU which basically states that after a specified period of time, the government/corporation will owe you the principal plus the interest for allowing the entity to borrow money from you. A simpler way to look at this is to think of yourself as a bank who goes out and lends governments/corporations money.

Since, you are lending to a government or a stable corporation, bonds are regarded as one of the safest securities that exist on the markets because the probability of a government defaulting on its loans is highly unlikely (though it has happened to numerous countries, numerous times but we won't dive into that now.) Since, the chances are relatively low, the reward of a bond is also very low. For example, you might see bonds with interest rates of 2%-3% indicating that you will only earn 2%-3% return on your principal which isn't much but if you are looking at a safe investment then bonds will work.

Wrapping Up

Julian is quietly sitting at this desk, smiling at the marvels of the asset class. The simplicity and the organization baffle him. "Asset classes" he thinks to himself "are useful in ways that I couldn't have imagined. They are organized through risk, reward and legal regulations which can help me quickly understand the basic premise of any security that may exist. In addition, I can look at an asset class as a whole and determine if I should investment in the asset class at all. Therefore, the characteristics of an asset class as whole can also help me determine whether I should invest or not. Ah! The Asset Class, what would I do without it?"

Julian could not have explained the importance of the asset classes better. Though this chapter only contains three asset classes, there are many more that we haven't touched on. Primarily because the constituents of these asset classes are slightly unintuitive at first sight and take a lot more examples to explain then simple Julian.

The primary purpose was for you to be introduced to topics such as speculation, stocks and bonds so when these topics are introduced in the future, they won't be such a surprise. If you have understood these topics and then it is time for you to move on to the next chapter which *really* deals with the thick of things. If not then, take your time to understand the topics and then move on. It is important for you to have a strong foundation, if you are to wander the markets alone.

Chapter 2

Stocks and Bonds

The NYSE is bustling with people moving, shouting and sometimes running. The graphs are moving upwards and downwards sometimes like the moods of the traders on the floor. As the tickers turn from red to green and from green to red, the traders hold their breaths for just a second to see what may happen next. The market makes a hodgepodge of emotions in a trader. Sure their calculations are correct and their analyses descriptive but even then they do not know exactly when the tides will change.

As the traders get their wits about themselves, Julian sits at his desk still marvelling about the wonders of the asset class but he has decided he needs to move on and learn more about the markets. The next topic Julian wants to tackle is that of stocks and bonds. He isn't exactly sure what they are but he has a vague understanding of them.

Before Julian goes anywhere, he needs to understand what exactly the markets are and how the markets function.

2.1   The Markets

The term "Markets" is used haphazardly to describe all the different types of markets that exist. For example "I'm going to be long oil and hope that the prices rise otherwise my position will be at a loss", this is something typical you hear from an investor and it sounds a little confusing at first but with a little insight it isn't.

Here we need to analyse the sentence itself and not the words that are being used in it such as "position" and "bull", they are not of paramount importance. What is paramount is the gist of the sentence which deals with the oil. If we recall from the previous chapter oil falls under the commodities asset class thus the investor must be talking about the commodities market. The other words that were used in the sentence will be discussed in the upcoming pages, be patient!

Generally speaking, a "market" is a place where buyers and sellers can meet in order to exchange goods/services. In the context of the Stock Market, it is where traders will meet in order to exchange stocks. There is also a bond market where, bonds are bought and sold. However, bonds are usually sold "over the counter".

Types of Markets

When a stock is first issued by a company, it enters the **primary market**, which is also known as the "new issue market". The primary market is simply a place where new securities are "connected" to buyers.

Primary Market: A market that issues
new securities on an exchange.

The main purpose of the issuance is to allow the company to raise funds for whatever needs they may have. The issuance is known as an Initial Public Offering. An **Initial Public Offering** (IPO) is the act of selling shares of your company to the general public for the first time. Those shares are distributed by an underwriting investment bank which has determined the price beforehand.

Underwriters, as they are commonly referred to, are investment banks that issue a company's stock for the first time. Their purpose is to buy the shares, at a discounted price, from the company and then resell the shares at the full IPO price to the public. The spread between the discount price and the IPO price is how underwriters make money. This is known as a firm commitment, where the investment bank will buy a pre-determined amount, resell it at full IPO price and then profit from the spread. Another way underwriters generate money is through the underwriting fees they collect in order to make the IPO.

Once the shares are bought by investors from the underwriting investment banks, the trading of those shares from one investor to another happens in the **secondary market**.

The secondary market is where the majority of trading takes place and the profits or losses made by investors during the trading of the shares does not directly affect the company itself. The most commonly known secondary market is the NYSE. The secondary market doesn't just exist for stocks but it also exists for other securities as well.

The Stock Exchange

The stock market is truly a fascinating place to be in and it does not matter where the exchange is located, be it Bombay or Tokyo, the feeling one gets when they step into an exchange is overwhelming.

There are two types of stock markets that exist around the world. The first type of market is an auction market such as the NYSE and the second type is an electronic market such as the NASDAQ. The main difference between the two types of markets is the fact that one is physical (NYSE) and the other is electronic (NASDAQ).

Since the NYSE is a physical stock market, you will see traders running around in open outcry about the stock they are selling or buying. Face to face interactions have their advantages and disadvantages. For one, the emotion of a trader when he/she is buying or selling a stock could be signal to help you adjust your position. Therefore, you not only have to absorb empirical data but also emotional data. This system has obvious disadvantages. For one thing, trades can be executed extremely quickly on a computer system and they can be done for cheaper. Furthermore, a computer system is extremely efficient to use because it saves time and energy. On an electronic exchange, traders only have to sit at a computer and click. They can execute numerous trades in succession whereas in open outcry, this may be difficult. Since 2009, the NYSE has removed a majority of the trading floor and has become a hybrid exchange by combing auction trading and electronic trading.

The NASDAQ, on the other hand, is purely an electronic exchange. The purpose of the NASDAQ is to connect buyers and sellers over the internet. As mentioned before, it makes trading, a whole lot more efficient and effective. For example, trading more than one security in a pure auction market would be rather difficult because you only have one mouth. Whereas the NASDAQ allows you to trade multiple stocks at the same time because it connects buyers and sellers quickly.

Bid and Ask

When traders are buying and selling a stock on the exchange, they are either *bidding* a price or *asking* a price respectively. The **bid** price is the price a buyer is willing to buy at and the **ask** price is the price the seller is willing to sell at. For example, Bob bids $10 on ABC which means Bob is willing to buy ABC for $10. By extension then, if Bob *asks* for $11 on ABC it would then mean that he is willing to sell for $11. Since there are a lot of people buying and selling stock at the same time, naturally there will be the highest price and the lowest price for a given stock. The difference between the two is known as the "bid – ask spread" or more commonly "bid – ask". For example, Bob is asking $11 for ABC and Jill is bidding $10, the bid – ask would be $1. In reality, there would be a variety of prices and therefore, the bid – ask would be between the highest price a buyer is willing to pay and the lowest price a seller is willing to sell.

The bid – ask is a great measure of liquidity. For example, cash is the most liquid asset on the planet and the bid – ask between two currencies is extremely low. Whereas, the bid – ask between stocks that have low market capitalization, known as small cap stocks, is generally high.

There is a natural intuition behind why a small bid – ask indicates good liquidity. Let's take again the example of cash and its bid – ask spread. We know for a fact that the bid – ask spread of cash is extremely low. Which means that investors are confident and have an agreement on the price of cash or a particular currency. Therefore, if an investor decides to sell currency or buy currency they can expect to gain money very quickly because there will be enough people buying or selling.

Let's take a counter example of a stock that has a large bid – ask spread. This means that investors cannot agree, even within acceptable range of numbers, on the buying and selling of the stock. Therefore, when an investor goes to sell their stock they will most probably not be able to sell because they do not have an acceptable price. Which means that the stock cannot be turned into cash very quickly or in other words, the stock is illiquid.

The liquidity of stocks is provided by Market makers (also known as specialists who now firms). Market makers are firms that provide a bid price and an ask price on a particular security. What's the importance of market maker you say? Well, suppose you are trading on a market but no one wants to trade with you, or with anyone for that matter. Everyone feels that the price is either too high or too low. If this happens, then the exchange cannot make money, because no transactions are happening. Therefore, market makers are employed to "create a market".

Market makers make money by benefiting from

the spread of a security. For example, if ABC's bid-ask is at $19.50/$20, then he/she can try to make a profit by benefiting from the spread that is $0.50. Suppose Jim is trading ABC and decides to sell ABC for $20. Since Jim can quote both the bid and ask, he turns around and bids $19.55. Now Jim's bid is the highest and he has effectively "created a market". If Jim "convinces" a seller for his new bid which is $19.55 then he has done, what is known as "making the spread". The difference between the two prices is now $0.45. Therefore, for every share he sold and every stock he bought, he made $0.45. If he sold 1000 shares then he would have made $450. It is important to note that once a money maker enters the market, he/she has to buy or sell at least 1000 shares. Therefore, Jim would have had to sell 1000 shares then "leave the market" to turn around and buy those 1000 shares back. The number of the shares that have to be traded by a market maker is dependent on the exchange they trade on.

Who Runs the Markets?

A common misconception among individuals is that the markets are "run" by a group of individuals or a supreme being who has strings attached to every stock that exists on the stock exchange. The simple truth is that no one runs the markets. The markets are "run" by the individuals that invest in various stocks and bonds and other financial securities.

For example, suppose there is a fruit market near your home where various fruits are bought and sold. If you went to the market would you think that the price of an apple is set by someone?

Of course not. The price of an apple is set by the supply and demand of the apples. Therefore, other than the consumer who is buying the apples, no one controls the apple market.

Factors that Effect the Markets

There are many factors that affect the market in various ways but for now, we will be talking about only three and we will come back for the others once we have gained a much deeper understanding of other material.

The first topic that we will deal with is market sentiment. Market sentiment is self explanatory but not without a few terms. The market sentiment is basically how investors are feeling about the direction of the market, whether it is generally going up or down. It is said that if the general direction of the market is going up then the market is **bullish** or is a **bull market**.

> Bull Market: A market, whose general trend is up.

If the market can go up then it can also go down and that is referred to as **bearish** or a **bear market**.

> Bear Market: A market, whose general trend is down.

You may have seen the famous statues in front of the Frankfurt Stock Exchange, where the metallic bull is looking into the eyes of the metallic bear. The statues are alluding to the concepts of bear and bull markets and the constant fight between the two.

Sometimes this fight can last for 25 years! These sorts of markets are known as secular markets. Suppose the market is currently bear and has been so for around 10 years, then it is called a "secular bear" market. That does not imply that the market only sustained a downward trend for ten years, rather the general direction of the trend was downwards for ten years. Therefore, a secular bear market may contain smaller bull markets during its trend downwards. The same is true for a bull market that has persisted for a number of years. The secular bull market will have a general trend that is going up. Therefore, just like a secular bear market, it may also contain smaller bear markets.

Often, we hear news reporters saying "The Nikkei 225 experienced a **rally** today"

> Rally: Short upward trend in a bear or bull market.

A rally, as stated in the definition, is a very short period of growth that generally happens within a day of trading. A rally in a bear market is called a "bear market rally", which is sometimes called a "dead cat bounce" because of the short bounce a dead cat gains and then quickly loses. Likewise, a rally in a bull market is known as a "bull market rally" but sadly it does not have named that is associated with a dead animal.

Indexes

The most common tool investors use to analyse the market or gain an overall feeling of the market is to compare their position with that of an **index**.

Index: A tool that measures the performance of similar securities. E.g. Nikkei
225, FTSE 100.

An index is like a tracking "machine" that tracks
the performance of similar securities and compiles
them to a number which represents that section
of the market effectively. Generally, indexes track
the top stocks in their respective stock exchanges.
For example, the Nikkei 225 tracks Japan's top 225
stocks that follow certain criteria. By utilizing these
indexes, investors can see the performance of the
top stocks and adjust their positions accordingly.
Furthermore, it gives the investor an opportunity
to test the general direction of the market. Even
though indexes are wonderful tracking tools there
are more specific tools that help us determine market sentiment.

The most commonly used market sentiment indicator is the Volatility Index (VIX), which is sometimes called the "fear index", it measures the 30 day
volatility of the markets. However, what is **volatility**?

Volatility: The measure of dispersion of
price over time of a security.

Simply, the volatility of a security is a measure
of the range of prices a security takes over time. For
example, if stock ABC has a low volatility therefore,
the investor can conclude that over a short period
of time, the range of values ABC can take, in either
direction, will be little. The opposite is true for a
security that has a high volatility. It can be stated
that if the volatility of a security is high then the

range of values it can take is large, in either direction. It is important to take note that volatility does not indicate the direction of security but rather the dispersion of prices over a short period of time.

The goal of the VIX is to compare itself to the S & P 500 index options and then to measure the expectation of volatility of the market over the next 30 day period. Since the index is called the "fear index" there is a popular saying among investors "When VIX is high, it is time to buy. When the VIX is low, it is time to go!"

A high VIX index indicates that investors are bearish and that the market is likely to turn bullish very soon. Therefore, buying when the prices are low can prove to be advantageous. Furthermore, if the VIX is high then it is likely that investors are over-confident in their positions.

The VIX is a common tool investors use to test market sentiment. Even though I have stated that if the VIX is low then the market is likely to turn bull that is not set in stone.

One of most important lessons to be learned in finance is that at the immediate present, no one can be indefinitely wrong but only be wrong in retrospect. However, it is possible that some trades are more sound then others but again, that does not make the other trades wrong. Why is this? It is because investing is heavily dependent on personal analysis. If a graph of the S & P 500 was shown to me and then shown to you, it is very possible that you and I will come to very different conclusions. Therefore, the tools that are used by investors are merely tools that aid the overall analysis and are not the analysis itself.

Economics Factors that Effect the Markets

Let's shift gears and talk about the economy as a whole. More often than not, the status of the markets is coupled with unemployment figures and interest rates.

Let's take a look at unemployment. What exactly is unemployment? I mean it is a very simple term to understand or *is it*? I should not be building up suspense, you already know what unemployment is but you are probably going to need to adjust your definition of it, just a little bit. Unemployment, as most people see it, is the number of people who don't have a job. But the important addition to this definition should be "... who don't have a job and aren't looking for one. Therefore, someone who isn't looking for a new job is not accounted for in the unemployment rate. For example, a student like me, who is writing a book, that may or may not pan out, is not accounted for in the unemployment rate because he is not looking for a job. But, a person such as a recently laid off factory worker who is looking for a job is accounted for in the unemployment rate. What does this have to do with the markets you ask? To say a lot would be an understatement.

Unemployment

The effects of unemployment are many because they effect the individual directly.

One of the more obvious reasons why unemployment is bad for the markets and for the economy is because of the simple truth: people without money cannot invest. It's that simple. If you had a job and were making enough money to feed your family, buy luxurious goods and go on vacation and *still* have money left over then you wouldn't have a problem investing money. And even if you didn't have all of these things, as long as you have the money, you can invest. By taking the main component out of the process stops you from investing. We can conclude that it is a lagging indicator or in other words, an indicator that shows the economy, which includes the market, is lagging.

Unemployment alone does not do too much damage to the markets because there are factors that are working against it such as interest rates and inflation. These factors go hand-in-hand and therefore, I like to call them the "economic trifecta". The economic trifecta are a group of concepts that, even if you didn't have anything else in your arsenal, you could still make reasonable assumptions about the state of the economy and by extension, the state of the markets.

The people rather the institutions that keep these factors in check are the central banks. These are the banks that generally carry the name of the country. For example, Bank of Canada (BoC) or Bank of Japan (BoJ) or in the United States, The Federal Reserve or more commonly "The Fed". All of the central banks around the world carry the same responsibilities, their job is to keep track of the unemployment rate, control inflation and to keep it low and control interest rates to sustain growth.

The central banks of each country have the power to control interest rates. A central bank has interest rates in place where other banks can borrow money. In other words, it is the rate that commercial banks borrow money at. Therefore, if the interest rates of a country were at 2%, for example, then commercial banks would have to borrow money for a 2% interest. While we pay the interest rate that we are most comfortable with, it is not a stretch to say that most people would not have difficulty in pay a 2% interest rate.

But suppose now the tides change and the interest rates are much higher, they are at an egregious number such as 10%! Then, as we have learned, commercial banks will have to borrow money at that rate. If commercial banks borrow money at that rate then they have to charge their customers even more to make money themselves. This would imply that consumers such as new home buyers or entrepreneurs will be very reluctant to borrow from the bank. Take for example the following scenario where I describe mortgage. Do note, however, that the mortgage I am about to describe is *the* most basic and is not used anywhere, in reality compound interest is used. Thus, scenario is an example and should be taken as such. This mortgage will last for 20 years, your principal or the money you "put down" is $100000 and your interest is $11%. Then that would mean that at the end of 20 years, you will be paying your principal multiplied by your interest multiplied by time or in short, $P * R * T$. That would mean that you would be paying $220000 in interest! That is $11000 a year and not to mention the fact that you are paying double your principal and then some. So, clearly you can see that high interest rates would be a huge turn-off for consumers everywhere. This leads to a cycle where if consumers are not buying then logically, sellers are not selling at an affordable price. Therefore, if sellers are not selling then there is no money that is being injected into the economy and therefore, the economy is not running smoothly or not running in a favourable position for growth.

Furthermore, the effect this has on the markets is horrendous. When interest rates rise, people tend to move towards interest bearing asset classes, for example, the fixed interest asset class.

Generally speaking, high interest rates indicate a bear market because as stated earlier it reduces growth. During periods of high interest rates the economy sees increases in inflation. Inflation is basically the increase in the cost of living.

Inflation and the Price of Bread

Remember last year? When you were buying that amazing loaf of bread that you just couldn't live without? It cost you $3 then, but now, it may cost you a little bit more maybe $3.50 or $4. At this point, you are just wondering "What in the world? My amazing loaf of bread is $3 no more!" That is when you know, inflation has hit you.

Aside from the childish story, inflation is a serious issue because it erodes the value of money. As explained in the very short story, something you bought last year most probably will be more expensive this year. The central bank works hard to keep inflation low because it encourages growth.

One of the main tools a central bank uses to measure the inflation of a country is the "Consumer Price Index" otherwise known as the CPI. The CPI is a "basket" of the most common goods and services within a country such as the price of our amazing piece of bread, eggs, milk and services such as transportation. It then calculates a numerical value for those basket of goods and announces them as the CPI of that year. CPI is only useful if you find the percentage increase/decrease from the previous year. Otherwise, the CPI is a unit-less number and does not carry much information. By measuring the percentage increase/decrease the central bank can determine the increase in inflation or the increase in the cost of living. For example, if the CPI in 2011 was 165 and the CPI in 2012 was 200 then, through simple math, we know that there was a 21.1% increase in inflation. A 21.1% increase in inflation would suggest that a good that cost $10 last year will cost $12.11 this year. Now, this may not seem like a substantial increase in prices but when you make the same calculations over a plethora of goods then the reality of inflation will hit you.

How is Inflation Generated?

The answer is not so simple and there is not a definite way to determine the relatively finite factors of inflation. The most common component that economists and investors can agree upon is the supply of money in the economy. When I said "inflation erodes the value of money", I implied in some ways that an excess of money can erode its value. Let's conjecture a small village whose population numbers around 500 individuals. Their trading system is not monetary rather is based on *quid pro quo* or in non-Latin words: The Barter System. The Barter System allows individuals in the village to trade one good for another. For example, Tom may trade two fish for one stone glass. The speciality of the village is that an apple is the most valuable item. If you had an apple, you can practically trade it for anything. The villagers regard it as a common denominator and an apple is pretty standard. Since an apple could be traded for anything, its value was high and therefore, it was a something everyone wanted. One day, one of the villagers found a forest that was filled with apples as far as the eye could see. The villager brought as many apples as he could carry back to the village. This increased the circulation of the apples even more than before. Not long after, the value of an apple began to gradually decrease and lost its position as the standard in the village. Now two apples may get you one piece of meat. The value of the apple had truly changed in a long period of time.

The scenario illustrates the effect of an excessive supply of money in the markets. Within the situation, the apple can be regarded as money. It was a standard form of trade within the village and it could be traded for anything without worry.

Within the scenario we don't know where the apples come from or who distributes them but in the real world, the central bank controls the supply of money through something called "Monetary Policy". The villager who found the forest of apples and put them into circulation is analogous to monetary policy gone wrong. The process has been grossly simplified. Monetary policy is complicated in its implications and furthermore, in its initiation. Therefore, it is beyond this book to explain fully what monetary policy implies but the gist of the idea remains in that it controls the supply of money.

In the situation, when the apples were let loose into the market economy, the value of apples decreased gradually. Therefore, the value of the apples eroded and therefore, the situation is analogous to inflation in the real world. The important word to remember is "gradually" because the supply of money does not quickly change like the flow of water changes when you quickly turn the tap from full to low or vice versa. The inflation that most countries are effected by takes years to come into full effect and therefore, can sometimes go unnoticed. But, there are instances where inflation gets out of control and reaches the point of hyperinflation.

Hyperinflation May Need Some Pills

Hyperinflation is the highest state of inflation and causes money to be almost worthless. We discussed that inflation is the increase in the cost of living or is something that erodes money. Well, simply put, hyperinflation erodes the value of money to the point where the value of money is almost nothing.

The Weimar Republic

The Weimar Republic is a classic example that is taught along with hyperinflation because it is one of the best examples in recent history. The Weimar Republic existed between the time after WWI and the rise of Hitler in 1933. One of the reasons behind the hyperinflation was because of the Treaty of Versailles, which was signed in 1919, and stated that the war was mainly Germany's fault along with the Central Powers including Austria and Hungary which was then the Austro-Hungarian Empire. Therefore, Germany had to pay the majority of the war reparations.

The reparations proved to be absolutely devastating for the German/Weimar economy. Soon after the implementation of the treaty in 1920, Germany experienced inflation and soon after hyperinflation. To put hyperinflation into perspective, workers were paid money in barrels because a few hundred Reichsmark would not do. As a matter of fact, money was so worthless that children played with bundles of cash instead of toys! There is one story of a customer who entered a café and ordered some coffee. When the coffee came its price had changed! Here's another example of how little money was worth. A passenger was a carrying a suitcase full of money and left it unattended to go to the wash-room. When he came back, he found that only the suitcase was stolen and the money was left alone.

The effects of hyperinflation are devastating to an economy and by extension to its markets. An economy can not only experience inflation but also *deflation*. Where inflation is bad for the consumer, deflation over a short period of time is good for the consumer because it decreases the cost of living.

The chief concern with deflation is that over the long term, it restricts businesses from doing trade effectively. During bouts of deflation, the currency of the country will weaken. The trade that takes place within the country will be severely affected because imports will cost more and the value of exports will decrease. For example, if you were an exporter of wood then the price you will receive for the wood will be much less than you received before. Since the currency of the country is weak, buyers will easily be able to buy the wood for less. Similarly, wood that you import from other countries will be more expensive because your currency is weak. Therefore, you will have to pay more money to get the same amount of wood that was much cheaper previously.

Deflation is not necessarily rare but it is certainly not common. The most common that is experienced by countries is inflation. As mentioned before, inflation is the general rise in the cost of living. Inflation is very interesting as it can be related to many aspects of finance. For example, inflation can be related to unemployment through what is known as the "Phillips Curve". In the short run, there is a trade-off, according to the Phillips curve, between inflation and unemployment where inflation and unemployment are inversely related. Imagine a graph downward sloping curve. With the x-axis as unemployment and y-axis as inflation. Therefore, as unemployment increases inflation decreases or vice versa, as unemployment decreases inflation increases. Do note, however, that this only applies in the short run or short term and has not been seen in the long run or long term.

Inflation, Interest Rates and Exchange Rates

An exchange rate is a fairly simple concept to understand with no strings attached. You may have been to the airport and probably would have decided to get the currency of the country you are travelling to. No matter which currency exchange "shop" you are at, there will be a sign in the front of the shop that will have the most common currencies and numbers beside them. Those numbers are, in fact, exchange rates. An exchange rate is how much of your own currency you can give to gain another country's currency. For example, the Canadian dollar (CAD), in recent times, has been exchanged for $1 CAD to $1.01 USD, therefore the ratio between $1 CAD is $1.01 or in other words, for everyone $1 CAD that you exchange, you will get $1.01 USD. Now, how much CAD is $1 USD? Let's do some simple math.

$$\frac{1 \quad CAD}{1.01 \quad USD} = \frac{x \quad CAD}{1 \quad USD} \tag{2.1}$$

I have set-up an equation here to simplify the process. The left side explains what we already know, that $1 CAD is equivalent to $1.01 USD. The right side is where the magic happens. On the right, we don't know how much $1 USD is worth in comparison to x CAD. If we cross multiply the denominator on the right side to the numerator on the left side and then divide, we get $0.99. Therefore, $1 USD is worth $0.99 CAD. Simple right? Let's do one more example, with different numbers. Even though you won't be required to do this, at any given time, it is important to understand literally how money is exchanged. So, suppose $1 CAD is worth $1.21541 USD. How much is $1 USD worth?

$$\frac{1 \quad CAD}{1.23541 \quad USD} = \frac{x \quad CAD}{1 \quad USD} \tag{2.2}$$

Once again, if we cross multiply the denominator of the right side to the numerator with the left side then we get a value for x of $0.822 CAD. Therefore, $1 CAD is worth $1.21541 USD and $1 USD is worth $0.822 CAD.

Exchange rates between countries vary and just as deflation affects exports and imports, among other things, so do exchange rates.

Exchange rates play large part in a country's economy along with inflation and interest rates as mentioned before. The aim of the central bank, along with unemployment, is to try and control these numbers, if you will. The main problem with controlling all three is that you can't and that is true for various reasons.

We have associated foreign exchange rates with imports/exports, interest rates with investment and inflation with the supply of money. The relationships that we have developed are central to understanding exactly why it is so difficult to maintain all three at once.

Suppose there are two countries initially and for simplicity let's call them Country A and Country B. The trade between A and B is simple. They maintain similar interest rates and their currencies are around ratios of 1 to 1. The inflation in both countries is also similar. In short, A and B are very similar countries so we will call them "The Originals". The Originals are minding their own business but now there is the addition of another country C. C is not very similar to The Originals but trade always occurs between The Originals and C. Now The Originals have to worry about their position because they have a new competitor.

Since C does not have similar interest rates, investors may be inclined to move to C to invest because the interest rates provided there prove to be more beneficial. Therefore, The Originals decide to change their interest rates to convince investors to stay. The change in interest rates causes inflation to rise and causes foreign exchange rates to fall. Ergo, imports and exports are now in jeopardy due to the fall in exchange rates and inflation has caused the cost of living to increase. Now the central bank decides to switch back its interest rates but this stops investors from flowing in. Therefore, the inflation decreases but foreign exchange increases, once again disrupting import/exports and cost of living.

Now imagine this happening with more than 20 different countries. Even though trade is splendid its consequences can be sometimes devastating if not handled properly. In the scenario, I said the first two countries were very similar in nature but this is very rare to see around the world. Most, if not all countries have different policies put in place to control different aspects of the economy. In the example, I only talked about the variance in interest rates but the case could be made for any other.

For example, if inflation begins to rise, the central bank will usually increase interest rates to discourage growth which would in turn reduce inflation. This is due to the fact that as the economy grows due to low interest rates, inflation increases. Remember, low interest rates encourage individuals/business to borrow money and spend. Thus, by increasing interest rates, the flow of money decreases or in other words inflation decreases.Thus, it is very difficult to control the group of three perfectly.

One of the main things, I want to stress throughout this book is that the markets are place for you to try new ideas and fail and to fail because it is *très important* to do so. Of course, you will lose money in the process and if you are not careful, lots of it but you will gain experience and in the markets, experience is paramount. The markets are one of the few places in the universe where probability is king. Like a physicist that uses Heisenberg's Uncertainty Principle, which states that it is impossible to know the momentum and the position at the same time with exact precision, investors and money managers cannot know absolutely where the electron or in this case the markets will be. They can only give their best estimate as to what might happen as a physicist can only give the best estimate as to where the electron may be in the near future.

Between sections we have talked about topics across the spectrum and I will not be surprised if you didn't pick up on all of it. Heck, I didn't pick up on all of it the first time either and I had to read them over a few times to fully grasp them. It is very important to understand why some of the concepts work and this is something I cannot stress enough. By memorizing, you are stunting your creativity and imagination and this couple is very important in finance. Therefore, I suggest that if you have not fully understood something, go back and understand it. Ask some questions while you are at it and research them later to gain more knowledge. Who knows? You may stumble upon something that you never knew existed.

Let's quickly summarize some of the few things we have learned over the course of the past 10 − 15 pages before we move onto the next topic. Firstly, we talked about the factors that affect the market, not all of them, yet, but the important ones for now. We said these were: inflation, interest rates, exchange rates and unemployment. The change in anyone of these factors causes another to change. Essentially, you should imagine four levers side by side and the move by themselves when one of them is tinkered. Secondly, we talked about market sentiment and the VIX. We said this was a great measure to determine how the market is "feeling" and assess the situation from there and that this was only a tool and not the entire analysis. Furthermore, we talked about indexes, bull markets and bear markets. An index we said was a tool that tracked something in the markets. A bull market was a market that was generally going up and bear market was the opposite, a market that was generally going down. So, we have successfully summarized the past 10-15 pages, albeit not in detail but rather decently.

2.2 Stocks, Finally

We briefly touched upon what a **stock** is in the previous chapter but did not define it. A stock is a portion of a publicly traded company.

> Stock: A type of security that signifies ownership in a corporation and represents a claim on a part of the corporation's assets and earnings.
> Investopedia.com

For example, a company decides to give a portion of their equity to raise funds. The concept is relatively simple because we are familiar with it in the real world. Suppose, you were a "publicly traded company" and you had 100% equity in your laptop. You wanted some money to buy something else so you decided sell a portion of your equity to a friend for some money. For about $50, you sold him 30% of the laptop. You issued to him a stock certificate that stated the aforementioned and received the funds, making him a shareholder. Thus, what you have done is sold a share in your laptop to your friend for some funds.

A stock certificate indicates to the receiver and verifies that they own the stock and furthermore, is in the records of the issuer that an issuance has happened. In addition, the stock certificate contains other valuable information such as the par value of the stock and the class of the stock.

Throughout my examples, I have talked about one share or stock being issued and how that affects the equity of a company by a substantial amount. But in the real world, that is not the case. Publicly traded companies issue massive amount of stock that number in the millions and sometimes in the hundreds of millions. Therefore, owning a small piece or even a hundred shares of a large corporation is going to have a negligible effect on the equity of the corporation.

Let's quickly go over the accounting aspect of a stock. We haven't dealt with the accounting aspects of any security yet but it will become prevalent in the upcoming chapters. On a balance sheet (a record of the company's assets, liabilities and the owner's equity) there is an order that must be followed which is determined by liquidity.

As we know, liquidity is how quickly something is turned into cash. In the assets category of a balance sheet, this is the way accounts are ordered. Therefore, in assets, cash will always go first for obvious reasons. In liabilities, however, the bank will always go first because they are to be paid first in the even of a bankruptcy. The liabilities section is then divided into the order in which creditors are paid. Since stocks represent an ownership in the business, they too are given priority in the event of bankruptcy, albeit not very high. Therefore, if a company goes bankrupt then each person will get money that is proportional to the amount of stock they hold.

Types of Stocks

More often that not we hear people referring to stocks but they do not indicate which type of stock they are talking about. Yes, there is more than one type of stock. Most commonly, we hear individuals talking about common stock and less commonly, preferred stock. If you guessed that there is inequality between these stocks then you would be absolutely correct. Meaning, both types of stocks have different advantages and disadvantages to them and therefore, what type you choose really depends on you. Not only are there two categories of stocks but there are categories within a category, e.g. categories within the preferred stock category.

Firstly, I want to talk about the preferred stock category and specialities. This is primarily because the category is rich with information and quite frankly more fun to talk about than the boring old common stock.

Preferred stock is given to the group of stocks that generally has precedence over dividends, is given the option to convert into common stock and the fact that they generally cannot vote in company policy.

The first concept we need to clear before we go anywhere is that of the dividend. The **dividend** is a portion of the profit that is given to a shareholder depending on many shares they hold.

> Dividend: A distribution of a company's earnings Investopedia.com

For example, if I own 100 shares of preferred stock and the profits that year are $10 000 then I will receive an x number of dollars for my shares in relation to the profit. The money each share receives is decided by the board of directors. This is most commonly known as "dividends per share" and if the dividend is based on a percent of the current market price then this is known as dividend yield. But the main question is "How does this make preferred shares special?" In one word: Precedence. Preferred shareholders receive dividends before any of the other shareholders or sometimes they could be the only class that receives dividends. This proves to be advantageous in the event that the company's stock does not gain value. Therefore the preferred shareholders can still earn money. It is important to note that large corporations rarely give out dividends because for the most part they reinvest the profits back into the company to keep increasing the funds.

One of two things can be done when a company makes a profit. Firstly, they can reinvest the profits to expand the company or they can distribute it through dividends to the **preferred shareholders** and sometimes to the **common stock shareholders**.

Preferred stockholders are also given the opportunity to convert their stock to common stock before a given date. The shareholder can, if they want, convert their preferred stock into common stock for whatever reason.

One of the major disadvantages to preferred stock and what sets it apart from common stock is the fact that preferred stockholders cannot vote in a company's policies or the election of the board of directors. The chief reason as to why this is done is because the company does not want to give all of its shareholders the right to vote. Remember, the primary reason why companies issue stock is to raise capital. By issuing preferred stock they are only obligated to issue dividends and not, necessarily give power to preferred shareholders, which give the company more control of what they can and cannot do.

The control of a corporation and its dealings is talked about in depth in the next chapter which is solely dedicated to explaining how corporations function. One of main topics that are discussed is the issue of power within a corporation and how it changes.

As I mentioned before, there are types within a type when it comes to preferred stock. Preferred stock is just a general name that is given to stocks that follow the three criteria I talked about earlier. A normal preferred stock is often called a "straight preferred stock" and a preferred stock that can be converted is called a "convertible preferred stock." Furthermore, it is possible for preferred stock to have special voting rights which allows the stockholder to be able to vote on special events but this is rarely the case.

In terms of the order in which dividends are paid and creditors are paid, the common stock comes right after preferred stock. Common stock is fairly simple to understand because it is stock that does not fall under the preferred stock category.

Common stockholders, first off, get dividends paid last and in the event of a bankruptcy their money is returned last – if there is any. More often than not, the money the company has to pay off the bank, their other loans and preferred shareholders runs out, leaving common stock shareholders with virtually nothing.

Within the common stock category are there are two classes of stocks: the voting class and the nonvoting class. The voting class gets to, obviously, vote. But what do I mean when I say "vote". After all, we are not talking about countries here but companies. Think of stockholders as citizens of a company. By buying stock for the company you are a part of it and therefore, you have a say in its operations, much like you do when you go to the voting stations. Thus, when a company votes on a major decision such as the election of the board of directors you have the right to vote on the decision. For instance, if Company A has been having a difficult year in the markets and decides their boards of directors are not adequate then they can vote on the decision to replace them. But unlike citizens in a country, not all stocks are created equal. Thus, only voting shares can vote while the others sit and watch. This gives common shareholders a capital advantage even if they don't receive dividends first. By having voting power, it allows them to govern the company. Of course, the shareholders do not get to govern the day to day because it would be very inefficient and counter-productive but again, they get a say in the company's major decisions.

So, what of the non-voting common stock? Nothing. They remain as they are – with seemingly no benefits. Non-voting shareholders get be a part of the company and win/lose money in the fluctuations the stock makes. This is main the reason why non-voting stock is less popular now. It simply has very few or almost no benefits.

Broker and Fiduciary

Over the course of the past chapter and in this one, I have been constantly been referring to the "investor". Before the invention of the NASDAQ, you could only trade through a broker. A broker is a company or a single individual that acts as the middle man between the buyer and seller. If you wanted to buy a stock, you would call a broker and they would quote you a price. A broker though, is not a fiduciary. The purpose of a broker is to get you to buy at all costs so they can make the most commission. Their job is not to necessarily help you. A fiduciary, on the hand, *does* help you. That means a fiduciary will tell you when to buy and sell and act in your best interest whereas the broker will not. Now, as you know, it not necessary for you to find a broker due to electronic exchanges such as the NASDAQ.

Growth and Value

All of the stocks that I have mentioned such as common stock or preferred stock also fall into two categories such as growth and value. To put simply, a growth stock is a stock that is expected to grow above average in comparison to the stocks in its category. On the other hand, a value stock is a stock that is undervalued contrary to its financials such as P/E.

Some Terminology

You may have heard financial analysts drop a few words here and there that seemed most confusing to you. Some of the terms are fairly easy to understand, while the others require a little more knowledge.

Finding the price of a stock is fairly simple nowadays and can be simply found through an online search. On the next page I have a graph and a table that one might commonly see when they are getting quotes from the internet. I have made up the company and the numbers, so do not pay too much attention to those rather try to think about what the numbers mean and how they relate to one another.

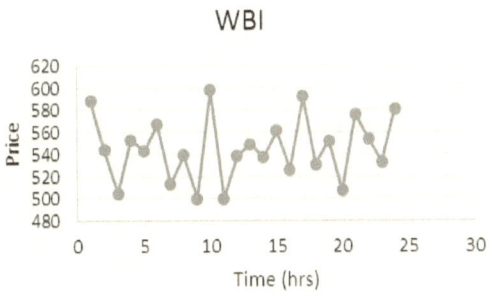

Figure 2.1: Shows the growth and decline of WBI

Open	512	P/E	21.0
Range	500–598	Mkt.Cap	100.5B
52 Week hi./lo.	456–612	# of shares	256m
VOL/Avg.	355458760/2914515	Beta	1.02
Ask	510.25	Inst. Own	45%
Div/Yield	–	Bid	511.25
		EPS	25.07

Table 2.1: Shows the various aspects of WBI

The two pictures I have provided are generally laid side by side or one is embedded into another. Seeing as how we have little space, we will have to make do with what we have.

The graph that has been provided is fairly self-explanatory, the x – axis represents the time which can either range from days to years and the y – axis represents the price of the stock. The graph I of "WBI" is over the course of one day and therefore, cannot provide too much information.

The first set of terms we will tackle are the terms that are on the left side of the card. These terms are more commonly known and are fairly easy to understand because most the definitions are exactly what you think they are.

The Easy Terms

The "Open" price is the price at which the stock opened at when the exchange opened for the day. You may have heard something along the lines of "Today, WBI opened at $512 and showed optimism." The "range" price and the "52 week high/low" are similar in that they give the range of the stock over the course of some time. The "range" price is the highest and lowest price of the stock over the day and the 52 week high/low is the highest and lowest price of the stock over a year. This is as simple as it gets, the range and 52 week high/low represent the range over a day or a year and the open price shows the price at which the stock opened.

Next on the list is "VOL / Avg." The "VOL" or Volume is the amount stock that has been traded over the day. For WBI this would be 354 587 60, the "Avg." is the volume over a longer period of time such as a month but more commonly over year. The VOL/Avg. can be used to determine the popularity of the stock. Furthermore, a stock that has a VOL/Avg. most probably has a low bid-ask spread because it is being more commonly traded. The VOL/Avg. is, naturally, a good indication of the scale of a company. Suppose, the VOL/Ag. is a large number then logically, it would mean that the company has issued a large number of stock and if that is the case then company must have had enough equity to distribute.

The ask price is something that we have already familiarized ourselves with and therefore we will not be spending time on it. Just in case you forgot, the ask price is the price at which the seller is willing to selling.

If you recall dividends are the distribution of profits and the "Div/yield" is exactly just that. It indicates the latest dividend that was paid out. The yield portion is just the percent that is derived from the current market price. For example, if Share A's market price was $100 and the dividend paid out was $10 then the Div/yield can be stated as 10% because 10% of the current market price is the dividend or in other words 1% of $100 is $10 – the dividend.

The Difficult Few

Now we are onto the harder column, we have completed the easy stuff and it's time for the slightly harder stuff. The numbers in this column are far more useful than the numbers in the left column but that is not to say that the left column is completely useless. The left column has its advantages but the right column gives more subtle information and allows the reader to analyse the stock better.

We'll start from the bottom, instead of the top, this time with Earnings Per Share or EPS. The EPS of a stock is used heavily by investors to determine the profitability of the company and to decide whether it is worth it to invest. It is one the most important factors in determining the price of a share. But, what exactly is EPS though and how is it calculated? We haven't talked to Julian, in a while why not pay him a visit?

Julian and the EPS

Julian is sitting in his black leather chair, which points to the door. On his desk are various financial statements and portfolios. A portfolio, by the way, is a collection of your investments. He has been looking into two companies that he has wanted to invest in for some time and wonders of the options he has to narrow this choice. His mentor had taught a few things and recalled a talk on EPS. He took out a meticulous book that gave him the information to everything financial. He opened up to the EPS section and poured over the details because it is a meticulous book. After ten minutes of reading, he learned that EPS means how much money a company allocates to its outstanding shares and that the calculation is done by subtracting the dividends from the profits and then dividing by the total number of outstanding shares. The process looked fairly simple to Julian so he decided to test it on the companies in question.

Timmy Turnip's Phones was a growing business that was located on the east side of Toronto. The business was quite popular among the locals and sometimes, there were people that were coming from out of town. In one year, the company had made a profit of \$500 000, had given out dividends of \$20 000 and had outstanding shares of 10 000.

Jamie's Gym was located on the other side of town and it too was making some business. Its price for membership was low and consequently its membership was high. Jamie's outfit had made a staggering profit of \$600 000, gave out dividends of \$10 000 and had outstanding shares of 20 000.

Julian looked at the books of both businesses

and quickly calculated the EPS for both them. Without the calculations, it would seem that Jamie is the better business simply because of the profits it made but that is not the case once the EPS for each business has been calculated.

It turns out that Timmy Turnip's business was the better business to invest in because its EPS was $48 whereas Jamie's EPS was only $29.5 in comparison. Here is how Julian calculated the EPS for both the companies. For Timmy Turnip's Phones he took the profit, $500 000 subtracted it from the dividends, $20 000 and divided by the number of outstanding shares, 10 000. This resulted in an EPS of $48. He did the same thing for Jamie's gym but just changed the numbers to arrive at $29.5 EPS.

By calculating the EPS of a company, Julian made a better judgement of which company to invest in. EPS is also important for something called "P/E ratio" or the "Price to Earnings Ratio". This ratio, as the name suggests, takes the current price of the stock and divides it by the EPS. The primary purpose of the P/E ratio is to evaluate the company against other companies in the same industry or compare against themselves against a historical P/E of their company.

Let's calculate the P/E for Timmy Turnip's Phone (TTP) and Jamie's Gym. TTP has a current stock price of $20 which is the same as Jamie's Gym. As we talked about earlier, to find the P/E we will take the current stock price, $20 and then divide it by the EPS which is either $48 or $29.5 for TTP and Jamie's Gym respectively. Therefore, the P/E for TTP is $0.41/$1 and Jamie's P/E is $0.67/$1.

Before, I explain what these numbers mean, try

and figure out what you think they might mean. Write it down on a piece of paper and check later if you are correct. This will accelerate your learning and enhance your critical thinking skills. Try your best to connect the dots as much as possible.

The P/E ratio in this scenario indicates that for TTP, every $0.41 that is invested $1 in earnings is gained. Likewise for Jamie's Gym, for $0.67 the investor expects $1 in earnings. As they say, numbers never lie and in this case TTP is clearly the better investment. Primarily because you have to invest less money to gain more, simple!

Suppose I had a company that had a low P/E earnings, then what does that mean? Well, we know that, a low P/E indicates that investors expect lower growth and a high P/E indicates that investors expect higher growth from the company. If you recall, I talked about factors that affected the markets and recall, I also said that were other factors, well here is one of them. Investors constantly use the P/E ratio to determine the growth of companies in relation to other companies. Therefore, if investors expect low growth from companies or in other words low P/E then the market may sour. By the same token, if the investors expect a high growth or a high P/E then the market may turn green.

Market Capitalization

Every now and then, people throw around the term "Market Capitalization" and they say something along the lines of "The Mkt. Cap for ABC just increased to $5b." This is a fairly simple statement and the term is used in a wide variety of contexts but this is the most common one. Market Capitalization is the amount of shares the company has ever issued multiplied by the current price of one share. For example, if ABC was selling at $5 and the amount of shares it had ever issued were 10 000 then ABCs market capitalization would be $5 * 10\,000 = \$50\,000$ and we would consider this company a small "cap" company.

There is not an exact definition of what a small "cap" company is but it is generally thought of as a company that has a market capitalization of less than $2b. There is also "mid cap" which is a market capitalization between $2b and $10b and a "large cap" which is over $10b.

These terms are used quickly to give a general size of a company. Large cap companies are, of course, very large in size because they have issued a large number of stock and the price of their stock is high or they have issued a small of stock whose price is incredibly high. By looking at a company and their market capitalization, an investor can see the "reach" a company has in the markets.

Market capitalization can be affected by many things but more often it is affected by the same things all the other statistics are affected by such as volatility, growth expectations etc. In addition, it is effected by **stock split?**

> Stock Split: The dividing or splitting of
> a stock to increase the amount of stock.

A stock split occurs when a company wants to increase the amount of shares they have without diluting the price of the share. For example, if ABC has 1000 shares and one share is worth $100 and they go through a stock split of 2 to 1, which gives them 2 000 shares, then the price of the stock will be diluted due to the extra amount of stock. Therefore, companies will adjust the price of the stock as well.

The basic principle behind stock splitting is to keep the market capitalization the same before and after the stock split. For instance, ABC has 1000 shares and they issue a 2 to 1 stock split which results in 2000 shares. The market price of the stock before the stock split was $10 and after the stock split the stock price of the new stock is adjusted to $5 in order to maintain the market capitalization. The market capitalization before the stock split was $1000 * \$10 = 10000$ and after the issuance the price was also 10000 because $2000 * \$5$ is 10000 therefore, the market cap has been maintained.

I want to very quickly talk about the inst. own percentage that is on the left column on page 54. This percentage indicates the amount of stock that is owned by institutions such as hedge funds and mutual funds. The interpretation of the statistic varies from person to person. One can say that if the stock has a large inst. own then the company is growing because mutual funds and hedge funds want to invest in it. But on the other hand, it could also mean that the company is a safe company and funds are investing in it to play safe. Thus, the percentage of inst. own and its interpretation is up to the investor.

Beta

Let's conjecture a situation where an investor wishes to see the volatility correlation between their pickings and some benchmark such as the S & P 500. How would they do that? They would either need to know statistics or they could refer to the "beta" of the stock. The beta of the stock indicates the volatility correlation of stock to a benchmark. Beta is a great way for investors to determine the current state of the stock in comparison to other stocks. For example, a stock that has a beta value of −0.5 is considered to be moving inversely to the benchmark. Suppose the bench mark is the S & P 500 and its general direction is up then that would mean our stock is moving down because its beta is less than zero. The value of the beta is not limited to a certain number in other words it has no upper or lower bounds but depending on the magnitude of the positivity and negativity of the beta, the magnitude of the volatility correlation is determined. For example, if ABC had a beta that was less than zero such as −0.05 then we know that ABC is inversely correlated with the benchmark. But due to the beta being so close to zero, we can say that ABCs trend downward is not strong inversely correlated to the benchmark. If the rate was to move further away from zero than the inverse correlation between the two would be even stronger. The beta value can, not only be below zero but can also be above zero. Generally the beta value lies above zero and below one. A beta value within that range indicates that the security is directly correlated with the benchmark. For example, the ABCs beta value is 0.5 which means that ABC is relatively correlated to the benchmark. If the benchmark were to be moving upward then so would ABC but that does not mean the benchmark influences ABC. Remember, the beta value only shows the correlation between the benchmark and the stock. If the beta is zero then there is no correlation between the stock and the benchmark and if the beta is exactly one then the stock and the benchmark are perfectly correlated. It is possible, however, that the beta be above one which would indicate that the stock is moving strongly upward/downward in relation to the benchmark.

The place where most people get confused is when I talk about direct correlation and inverse correlation. These terms do not imply that both the benchmark and the stock are moving upward or that benchmark is moving upward. Direct correlation does not imply that the stock and benchmark are both moving up and inverse correlation does not imply that the stock is moving downward while the benchmark is moving upward. It can be very possible that the stock is moving up and the benchmark down and this can very well be classified as an inverse relationship. Furthermore, the benchmark and the stock could be directly correlated and they could be moving down. Therefore, there is no implication in the names that either the stock or the benchmark is moving up or down. Thus, one should not come to an arbitrary conclusion that is dependent on the name.

Combing all of the statistics that we have learned over the past few pages, you should be able to now analyse stocks to certain degree of expertise, albeit not as good as a professional such a stock broker but you should be able to analyse them better than the average person.

The things you have learned about stocks should not end because the world of stocks is massive and entire books are written upon them in great depth, instead, it is now your responsibility to go out and explore the unknown. There are numerous websites that offer virtual stock markets where users can invest virtual money and pick stocks and try to predict the outcome. This chapter is not over yet because we have yet to discover bonds but before you move on, go over some of these concepts again and understand the principles behind them. There is no use in memorizing any of the information you have acquired because applying memorized information only helps with specific cases and not all cases. Try to develop a method that will define your style. It's difficult to see two people with the same investing strategy or the same opinion, always, on stocks or the market in general. It is paramount to understand that there is no such thing as being right or wrong in the moment in analysing the markets. You can only be wrong retrospectively. Therefore, go out there and test your skills and see if you have actually learned something.

Now we move onto the world of bonds which is slightly less exciting but fascinating nonetheless.

2.3 Bonds

There are two types of people in the world, risk takers and those that like to play it safe. No one can say that one is better than the other because a contest cannot be made out of it. The eternal fight between risk and reward is exemplified by deciding between a bond and a stock. Stocks, as we have talked about, are riskier investments in comparison to the bond and if you recall from the first chapter bonds are safe investments because they are backed by a corporation whose credit rating is excellent or by a government but most bonds are backed by governments.

Bonds are primarily used by investors to mitigate risk in their portfolios. Since bonds are safe investments, investors can expect them to survive a bad day or for that matter long periods of bad days. The portfolio as a whole will not suffer too much damage with the bonds in it.

Like stocks, bonds are just as complex and one could argue even more complex. Bonds give us an extremely good look at the economic status of the government to which they belong. There are numerous types of bonds, like stocks and there are many facets we must explore.

Bond Basics

Just in case, you do not recall what exactly a bond is, let's recap. A bond is a government issued IOU which is issued to raise money. Corporations do not always issue bonds and are not known to do so but from a company's perspective it is a great alternative to stocks if you want to raise money without giving away equity. As you know, a corporation can raise capital in two ways; they can either give equity in return for money or they can ask for money and promise to pay it back in the future for interest. The latter is exactly what a bond is. It is a promise to pay back money in the future for interest. In addition, in the event of a bankruptcy the issuer is obligated to sell its assets in order to pay you back. As a result, it can be said that bonds tie assets down.

As I mentioned, bonds are more often issued by governments for numerous reasons such as war or to fund projects that otherwise will not have funding. You may have learned in history class the issuance of war bonds during WWI and WWII and your teacher may have even shown you posters that simply said something along the lines of "Buy war bonds!" They were not too creative with these posters but the point was that during those times the government needed extra money to fund the war effort and the only way they could get it was through people and thus through bonds.

As mentioned earlier, bonds are a safe investment because they are backed by a government but that is not always the case because there are some governments whose credit rating, a topic that we will discuss later, is low and consequently they are not very reliable in paying back the money owed.

Components of a Bond

Every bond has components that are essential to understanding how the bond works. There is specific terminology that is used by radio show hosts or the finance world in general. Without knowing these terms, it is very easy to get lost, thus this section should be paid particular attention to.

Face value

When a bond is issued the principal that is required is called the **face value** or the par value of the bond. Depending on the type of bond, the face value can range from a hundreds of dollars to thousands of dollars. The most common mistake that is made is to mix face value and the price of the bond. The price of the bond fluctuates through its lifetime whereas its face value doesn't. There are two terms that commonly associated with the face value and they are discount and premium. When the price of a bond is less than its par value it is known as a discount bond. On the other hand, if the price of the bond is above the face value then that bond is known as a premium bond.

Coupon

Since a bond is like an IOU or a loan of some sort, it must have an interest rate or in bond terms a **coupon**. A coupon is the interest rate that is associated with the bond and is either fixed or is floating. Fixed interest rates are fairly easy to understand because the interest rate remains the same throughout its lifetime and therefore, it is easy to calculate the yield, something we will talk about shortly. Furthermore, it makes the bond predictable in that it is easy to map out the payments that may come annually or semi-annually. The payments do not have to be paid annually or semi-annually, sometimes they may be paid every quarter or every month but commonly they are paid semi-annually.

Suppose the principal for a bond is $1000 and the coupon is 5% and it pays annually. Then the calculation is fairly simple, ever year the bond will pay 5% of $1000 which is $50. The situation is different if the rate is a floating rate. A floating rate, at the heart, is a rate that changes because it is pegged to the market which causes the interest rate to change. The main disadvantage is if you are going to hold onto the bond to the end of its lifetime then it will be difficult for you to predict how much interest you will gain at the end. But more often than not, bonds are bought and then sold like stocks in order to gain a profit.

Maturity

For the past few paragraphs, I have been talking about the life of a bond but believe it or not there is an actual term that is used to refer to the lifetime of bond and it is known as the maturity date. The **maturity date** is the date when the bond will expire and the issuer will have to pay the principal back. The maturity can range from one day to thirty years and generally the longer the maturity date the higher the coupon on the bond. The logic behind this is very simple. It is easy to predict the price of a bond or anything for that matter when the time frame is small. With short time frames, the variables that are "entering" and "leaving" are small and predicting them is not too difficult. If the time frame is expanded to, let's say, ten years then it is difficult to judge what may happen. Suppose, I asked you to forecast your life with a time frame of the next 10 minutes. You will not have trouble telling me that nothing much is going to happen to you. Suppose, I changed the time frame from ten minutes to ten years then that will be a whole other story. You will, undoubtedly, have a difficult time telling me what may happen to you. The analogy extends to bonds; the price of the bond is predictable with certain precision within a short time frame but over a longer period of time, the calculation will lose precision and will be more difficult to execute. Therefore, bonds with long maturity dates will have higher coupon rates as an incentive to investors and lower maturity dates will have lower coupons.

Yield

Along with the maturity date of a bond, the yield a bond provides is of paramount importance. The yield of a bond indicates the return on the bond. There are two types of yields that exist, the first one being **simple yield** and the second one being the **yield to maturity** which is more commonly used. The simple yield has a very simple calculation which is to take the current coupon and to divide it by the current price of the bond. For example, if I bought a bond whose coupon was 10% and its price was $100 then I would simply divide the coupon by the price and I would gain $10 because 10% of $100 is $10 therefore the yield is 10%. If the price of the bond decreases then the yield grows. For example, if the price of the bond decreases to $50 then the yield will go up to 20% because the coupon price remains the same and the price is changed to $50. Therefore, the calculation is $10/$50 * 100 which is 20%. Conversely, if the price of the coupon increases then the yield will decrease. For instance, the price of the bond increases to $120 then once again, we divide the coupon by the price, $10/$150 * 100, which gives a yield of 6.67%. Thus, from our examples we can conclude that an increase in price leads to a lower yield and a decrease in the price leads to a higher yield. By using the yield calculation, we have a good measurement of how much a bond is expected to return. Unfortunately, the main problem in using this calculation is that it is not comprehensive and is very rarely used by professionals.

Yield to Maturity (YTM) is the weapon of choice for most investors because the statistic includes a variety of factors that make the statistic more accurate and reliable. Though, that is not to say that simple yield is not reliable but rather simple yield is less reliable. YTM takes into account factors such as coupon payments to the maturity date. The calculation of YTM is slightly cumbersome and therefore, will not be explored thoroughly. Though the basic premise of the calculation is fairly simple to understand. The idea is to take into account factors such as present value, which is just the current worth of money for future income (more technically, future cash flows), coupon payment, face value and the total time. Once these variables have been found, they are plugged into a formula which looks something like this:

$$ApproxYTM = \frac{C + \frac{F-P}{n}}{\frac{F+P}{2}} \qquad (2.3)$$

The reason why the formula states an "approx. YTM" is because the YTM has to eventually equal the price of the bond and therefore requires trial and error and is usually done by a computer or a calculator. By utilizing the YTM, an investor can determine whether the bond is worth anything to them with relative precision.

Credit Rating

The first fact we learned about the bond was that it was an IOU and therefore, logically, the credit of the debtor would come into question. How can we know with certainty that the debtor will repay our money on time? This is where credit ratings come into play. Credit ratings, to put simply, are letter grades that are given to institutions, countries and securities such as bonds that depict the likely hood of a corporation or government defaulting on their loans. Credit ratings are a sure fire way to easily determine if the debtor will be able to pay money back.

The highest level of credit that can be given is AAA but this varies depending the credit agency but they all use three A's in some way shape or form e.g. Aaa. By having the highest credit rating, the corporation/country is indicating that they are *extremely* safe and are reliable enough to invest in. The scale moves from AAA to default and in between are ranks such as BBB+ or CCC. Generally bonds that are in the C range are considered junk because of the high risk they carry which is almost paradoxical considering that bonds are supposed to be one of the safest investments if not *the* safest. Due to their relatively high risk, junk bonds provide high reward and are popular amongst risk investors.

Countries and Credit Ratings

Countries are also given credit ratings the same way bonds are given ratings. The credit rating of a country determines its ability to pay off its debts and therefore, gives the investors an insight into the country's economic well-being. But that is not to say that a country that has a high credit rating is doing well. The only thing the credit rating indicates is the likelihood of the country paying off its debts.

Generally, high yield rates indicate a low credit rating, something I hinted at when we talked, briefly, talked about junk bonds. Suppose, I have a $100 bond that has a 5% coupon and has been issued by BondLand, a country that likes to raise capital through bonds. Recently, BondLand has been finding it difficult to pay off its debts and has consequently had its credit rating decreased. Due to the credit rating decrease, the price of the bond has also decreased to $80 and has therefore, increased your yield to 6.25%. Thus, the relationship is simple, a decrease in credit rating correlates to a high yield and vice versa. We can verify this by extending from what we already know from junk bonds. Junk bonds have credit ratings that are low and yield that is high. By having this knowledge, an investor can determine, with relative precision, the credit rating of a country. If the bond of a country has a yield that is, for example at 7%, then the investor can assume the country has a relatively low credit rating e.g. B.

Market Price

In the previous section, we discussed the influence of credit ratings in the bond market and how a decrease in rating influences the price of the bond. The logic for buying/selling at a discount is simple. The likelihood of the debtor paying off the debt has decreased and has therefore, caused the price of the bond to decrease. This is one of the main factors that effects the price of bonds in the market. Bonds that are bought at a premium are bought because their credit rating is good or has gotten much better or because they are expected to pay out more in the future. Both of these factors affect the price of the bond but above all, the interest rates that exist in the economy determine the price of the bond the most.

When the interest rates in an economy rise the price of bonds will decrease because of the decrease in safety (this is simplified, the specifics are too technical for the book). Likewise, when interest rates fall the price of the bond increases.

Remember that the prevailing interest rates in the economy are essential to understanding exactly how the bond functions, when it comes to pricing and otherwise. The main purpose of a bond for an investor, is to act as a cushion against any unwanted damage. If interest rates are high, then there is an indication that the bond is risky and therefore, will not cushion any unwanted damages but may be the unwanted damage itself.

Types of Bonds

Like stocks, there are numerous types of bonds and in fact, there are more types of bonds then are types of stocks. For example, for every level of government from municipal to federal, there is a bond in addition to corporate bonds and zero-coupon bonds.

Within the spectrum of federal bonds, there are three bonds that exist. These three bonds include the T-bill, Treasury note and the Treasury bond. The T-Bill is technically not a bond because of its short maturity date which is less than a year but nonetheless, it has the same characteristics as a bond such as the maturity date and yield. Instead of being traded on the bond market, it is traded on the money market, a market for short term securities such as T-Bill and commercial paper.

The T-bill works slightly different in terms of interest payments because of the process in which it is sold. The bill is sold at a discount price or in other words it is sold at a price that is below its par value. For example, if the T-bills par value is $1 000 then it will be sold at $900 but just like a normal bond the bill will pay the par value at its maturity. The interest is calculated from the difference between the par value and the discount price which is then divided by the discount price. For instance, a bond that has a par value of $1 000 and the discount price is at $900, the interest that we would earn is 11.1% because ($1 000-$900)/$900. Let's take another quick example, a bond has a par value of $5 000 and a discount price of $4800. The interest payment on this bond would be 4.167% because ($5 000-$4 800)/$4 800. In this respect, T-bills are very different but the terminology that is used when referring to the T-bill is the same. For example, the "pay day" for the bill is still called the maturity date and the yield of the bill is still called the yield.

The note, on the other hand, is considered a bond in all respects and has only been given a different name because of its range in maturity date. The maturity dates for all notes range from over one year to less than ten. Other than the maturity date, Treasury note does not differ from any other bond. The Treasury bond however, has a longer maturity date. The maturity date can range from over ten years to thirty years. Below is a table that illustrates the maturity dates of Treasury bills, notes and bonds. The t refers the maturity date of the "bond".

Type	Maturity (Yr.)
T-Bill	$t < 1$
T-Note	$1 < t < 10$
T-Bond	$10 < t < 30$

Moving down the scale, we encounter the municipal bond which is, obviously, issued by a municipal government. The main purpose for issuing municipal bonds is for municipalities to raise funds in order to fund projects within the municipalities. In some countries, such as the United States, municipal bonds are exempt from federal and state taxes, which proves to be advantageous for anyone holding a municipal bond.

Credit Ratings and Corporate Bonds

Credit rating is extremely important when it comes to government bonds. A government bond is only worth buying if the credit rating is nearly indestructible. If the bond does not carry a high credit rating then it is useless to most investors, as mentioned earlier, because it could prove be damaging to their portfolio rather than cushion any losses that might occur. Credit rating on the corporate scale is not extremely important or as important as on a government bond because it is expected that a corporate bond will have less than AAA credit rating.

Corporate bonds are issued by corporations to raise funds without trading equity. Usually corporations issue stocks to raise capital but that is not always the best option and therefore, issuing bonds is a great alternative. Investors who invest in corporate bonds have the opportunity to redeem their bonds before the maturity date if they hold a callable bond and are able to convert their bonds into stock if they have a convertible bond. This is analogous to convertible stock, in that it can be converted into another security which is specified by the stock certificate. The central distinction between the two is that one converts to a wholly different security whereas convertible stock converts most often to a different tier in the stock hierarchy such as common stock.

Considering a corporation is not a government (obviously) the risk is more which reflects in the credit rating. In the event of a bankruptcy, creditors such as bond holders are paid first and in that respect investors are safe. But if the corporation is in risk of default, their credit rating will be junk anyway and investors will, most often, be deterred away from those bonds.

Zero Coupon Bond

Up till now, we have only discussed bonds that have coupons but it is possible to own bonds that do not have coupons at all. These bonds are known as zero-coupon bonds. Zero coupon bonds, as the names suggests, have no coupon or zero coupon. These bonds are sold at a discounted price and come maturity are paid face value. For example, a zero-coupon bond with a face value of $1000 could be sold for discounted price of $700 and upon maturity date, the face value, which is $1 000, will be paid. Therefore you have gained a profit of $300. Comparing this to a coupon bond can lead to various conclusions. For example, if we had a coupon bond with a face value of $1 000 and coupon of 5% and maturity date of ten years. Our interest over ten years would amount to $500. Now if we bought a zero-coupon for $700 whose face value was $1 000 and its maturity was same as our coupon bond then we would only make a profit of $300 instead of the $500 we would be making with the coupon bond. Conversely, we could have a coupon bond that pays less than a zero-coupon bond.

The Issuance of a Bond

We talked, during the earlier part of the chapter, about the issuance of stocks through underwriting. Depending on the type of bond, the issuance of it varies. For example, corporate bonds are issued through underwriting just as stocks are.

Corporations find investment banks that are willing to write the bonds and distribute them. The process is very similar to the issuance of a stock except it is not called an IPO. Just as in stock underwriting, banks bear the responsibility of not being able to sell the bonds. For example, if $1 000 bonds were to be distributed and only $500 were sold, then the investment bank would be responsible for them. As in stock underwriting, the investment bank will charge a fee that for the issuance.

The issuance of government bonds is slightly different. Government bonds are not underwritten but are sold in an auction. The issuance of a bond is not a hyped event in contrast to an IPO of a well-known company. This is primarily because bonds are seen as safe investments and don't exactly get someone's adrenaline pumping. Consequently, if you are not in the "game" then there is a high chance you will not hear about it.

2.4 Wrapping up Stocks and Bonds

Over the course of this chapter we have covered numerous topics that have ranged from how the markets function to the constituents of the markets such as stocks and bonds. The function of the markets is something that is understood but not very well. Often times, economists and the like are surprised by the turns an economy takes or are astounded when the market hits new highs and new lows. They try to predict, to the best of their ability, the direction and the state of the economy but as I said, within the present moment no one can be absolutely correct when it comes to the market and therefore, everyone should take chances because the markets are one place where that is possible for anyone.

The constituents a market holds, whether it is stock or bond, are equally curious and surprising in their abilities. Even though bonds may seem like dull investments, the logic and basis of the creation is something to be marvelled. It is important when learning about the markets to *really* understand the nature of the security and its purpose. By understanding the nature and its purpose and by *truly* doing so, you are opening your mind to a whole range of possibilities you may have not seen before. Likewise, for stocks, their intentions and the statistics that come with them are truly fascinating because they tell a story. The story may not have been happy or sad but it definitely is informative. Finding the relationships between statistic A and statistic B is at the heart of stock analysis and whether you are an investor or a curious reader, finding relationships between A and B is joyous.

I encourage the reader to explore each area separately and beyond this book. Try to develop new ways of analysis or try to develop a method for analysing statistics or events. Be imaginative and creative because both are at the root of finance and the markets.

Chapter 3

What is a Corporation?

After Julian made his "Chorniator", which happened to be a success, Julian decided to buy the investor's portion of his company and tried to attract other investors, which proved to be difficult.

When Julian was in a partnership with the private equity investor, he had an unlimited liability while the private equity investor only had a limited liability. This meant that in the event of a bankruptcy, Julian was responsible for paying all the debts whereas Jim would be only liable to the amount he invested. This proved to be severely disadvantageous to Julian because after all, if Jim invested in the company he was a part of it and should be equally responsible.

Another aspect that bugged Julian was the fact that it was difficult to raise capital. After Jim invested in the Chorinator, raising capital became difficult because Julian had to find new partners. If new partners were sought then Julian would have to give up a portion of his portion, for example 20%, which would mean Julian had only 40% left over and therefore did not control his own company.

The problems with this partnership were many, raising capital one of them and he decided to take action by first talking to his mentor, George.

Julian and George met at the same old, rustic diner were they always met and ordered some coffee. Julian explained to George the problem he was facing and asked him, what he should do about it. For George the answer was simple "why not form a corporation?" Julian thought "why not?" but there was one problem, Julian did not exactly know what a corporation was. As a matter of fact, Julian had very little knowledge on corporations. All he knew was that corporations were a group of people with investors and shares.

Forming a corporation without knowing what exactly one is, can prove to be rather risky. Therefore, before Julian forms his corporation, he must figure out the ins and outs of a corporation.

Apart from Julian's adventures, this chapter is will be relatively short, in comparison to the previous chapter, which by the way lasted from page 25 to page 80! The purpose of this chapter is to clear up some misconceptions and to introduce the structure and the advantages and disadvantages of corporation. Furthermore, understanding the central aspects of a corporation will allow you to make more informed opinions.

3.1 What's a Corporation?

Julian's definition was slightly correct but very vague. A **corporation** is a group of individuals that come together and form a legal entity and construct a business.

> Corporation: A legal entity that is separate and distinct from its owners. Investopedia.com

For example, when a few individuals with similar ideas come together to form a business, they generally decide to make a corporation because of the advantages that come with forming a corporation. Furthermore, a corporation provides the owners with limited liability which greatly reduces personal risk. Forming a corporation allows the owners to raise capital much more easily than through a partnership, which puts personal liability for everyone that invests. This is in stark contrast to investors in a corporation who are only liable for what they invest.

Aspects of a Corporation

As I mentioned earlier, a corporation is a single legal entity which implies that the corporation is like a human except it is not alive and does not have certain other rights but otherwise, can be charged for criminal crimes and can also sue for human rights violations.

Being a legal entity, a corporation can survive long after the original owners have passed away through the shareholders that hold stock in the company. Conversely, a sole proprietorship and a partnership can only exist as long as the owners are living or if the owners pass off their stake to their children or otherwise.

Furthermore, because of the limited liability aspect, investors are more likely to pour in considering the business is profitable. This increases the chances of the corporation expanding more than a sole proprietorship or a general partnership.

Advantages and Disadvantages of Corporation

Corporations are all around us and they exist because they have some benefits otherwise, who would start a corporation? Some of the advantages we have already touched on and we will now go more in depth, to give you a full understanding of why people prefer corporations over alternatives.

We talked about dissolution briefly in the previous section and if you recall corporations can exist long after the original owners have died and this is completely true. They can exist as long as the corporation has stockholders. Remember from the previous chapter that a shareholder is someone who holds equity in the corporation. Therefore, as long as someone is holding equity, the company will exist. This is usually known as perpetual existence. A corporation has the ability to exist *ad infinitum* because it is a separate legal entity.

I cannot stress enough, how important it is for a corporation to be legal entity because every advantage and disadvantage surrounds this notion. Though, what does a separate legal entity mean?

Suppose, you procreated a baby. This baby, will have certain rights and freedoms. A corporation is similar to making a baby but unlike a baby, a corporation is not fully considered a person and therefore does not achieve "person hood". However, a corporation is considered to be its own "thing". Therefore, the assets that it owns are owned by *it* and not the shareholders, more on that later. Therefore, a corporation being a separate legal entity, it can exist forever since it exists on its own. However, a corporation can go through dissolution if it has violated some laws or has gotten too big in which case it will be broken down into smaller parts e.g. Standard Oil.

Being a legal entity, the debt a corporation incurs belongs to the corporation itself and not the investors. This is known as a limited liability. Limited liability allows investors to invest freely because the maximum amount of money they could lose is the investment that they made. This is in stark contrast to sole proprietorship or a general partnership because in both of these business types, the owner has unlimited liability. Unlimited liability puts the owner's personal assets on the line in the event of a bankruptcy to pay off creditors. Therefore, capital is easy to raise.

Since investors are not worried about losing their personal assets, they will be willing to invest in any company they feel will profit. Imagine, I asked you to invest in a company that required you to put personal assets on the line in the event of a bankruptcy. You would think that is an absurd idea! Why would you invest money *and* take the risk of losing personal assets if the company fails? Thus, limited liability is one of the only logical steps to take in order to raise capital effectively.

By extension, we can say that if more investors are coming in then the business is expanding. Therefore, one of the advantages of having a corporation is continual growth due to new investors. This being said, if the flow of investors or the flow of capital decreases then business will see a decline in growth. The process is simply *quid pro quo*, if one increases then so will other and vice versa.

Taxation - a Disadvantage

As we move into the disadvantages of a corporation, it is important to note that there are subtle advantages that are not mentioned, for example, certain tax advantages that corporations receive. This not true in all countries but in North America it is very evident. Along with the tax breaks that most corporations receive, they are also subject to double taxation which makes taxes a double edged sword.

Double taxation is not double taxes as in twice the normal tax, you would have to pay if you were a corporation. For example, if the tax rate were 15%, it is not double that amount rather double taxation is when the corporation is taxed on the profits and the shareholder is taxed on the dividends he/she receives. This is not the case around the world. At its root, double taxation is just the use of two or more taxes on a corporation. For instance, a corporation may be taxed on its profits and then taxed via sales tax. Ergo, double taxation can be quite the hassle if its a substantial amount for both the corporation and its shareholders. This is one of the reasons why entrepreneurs are reluctant to start a corporation.

Starting a corporation, in itself, is a disadvantage. The logistics of starting a corporation requires the use of a lawyer, which as you know can be quite expensive. Furthermore, depending on the state or province, the fees for starting a corporation vary. In addition, corporations receive a charter from the state/province that verifies and indicates various details such as its founders and objectives. For individuals who are low in capital and live in a state/province/country that has a high fee for starting a corporation, this can be a burden.

3.2   The Levels

Some corporations die as quickly as they are born because, in truth, corporations require maintenance which includes working in/as a team. More often then not, you will see a corporation that has more than five head positions, with each commanding a different portion of the company. Therefore, if the heads cannot come together to make decisions or come together in order to determine the path for the corporation, they are very likely to fail and put the shareholders in jeopardy.

The most important person in the corporation is the shareholder because without the shareholder, the corporation is not a corporation by definition and otherwise. It is the duty of every executive, especially the CEO, to "wow" the shareholder because (1) they want to keep the shareholders they have and (2) to bring new investors in. Consequently, one can say the top of the corporate pyramid is the shareholder.

As we know, from the previous chapter, the shareholder has certain rights such as electing the board of directors. The board of directors (BOD) are basically an extension of the shareholders. Since all of the shareholders cannot be overseeing the company, they elect the BOD to do it for them. Here is where common shares come in handy. Remember, for simplicity sake, only common shares have the power to vote, as a result, they govern the path of the company. The BOD come in all shapes and forms and have the responsibility of electing the CEO or Chief Executive Officer.

There are two types of directors: the inside director and the outside director. The inside director, for example, is someone like the CEO of the company. Inside directors are employees, shareholders, or officers of the company and have fiduciary duty towards the company. In other words, like a financial advisor, who is required to act in the best interest of the shareholder/company. By deduction, outside directors are individuals who are not employees of the company. They are elected to provide a different insight on the company's operation.

Suppose, you are working with a team of people who are trying to solve a complicated math problem and you and everyone within the team has tried every approach *they* know. You have essentially and sadly acquired tunnel vision which is keeping you from solving the problem. When all else fails you will ask someone to help you. By having a person who has not yet seen your thought process, they will be able to pitch their own ideas as to how to go about solving the problem. It may happen that they come up with an entirely new idea to solve the problem. This scenario is analogous to a corporation; substitute yourself with inside directors and the math problem with a corporation. Therefore, the outside helper or the outside director is very important to solving problems and keeping things in check. The combination of the inside director and the outside director is what makes the BOD and keeps the company running fluidly. The BOD is also responsible for appointing the chairman. The chairman is the "leader" of the BOD and oversees its meetings etc. In addition, the BOD also appoints a CEO.

CEOs are usually the face of the company. Every time you turn on the news, you most probably see the CEO, who is either trumpeting growth or restoring faith. More often than not, we see CEOs who are charismatic and extroverted and sometimes this is necessary. When investors look at a company, they are not only evaluating its financials but they are also looking at the individuals governing the company. If the CEO or CFO (Chief Financial Officer) comes off as weak then investors may see that as a turn-off.

The corporate ladder consists of various levels, three of which we have already talked about e.g. stockholders, BOD, CEO. On the next page, I have a pyramid that shows the different levels. The top of the pyramid exhibits the most power and naturally the bottom has the least.

3.3 Conclusion

Even though this chapter was short, we have managed to cover some decent ground. No topic in finance can ever be summarized within the few pages of book but I have tried my best to take the most important and relevant parts about corporations.

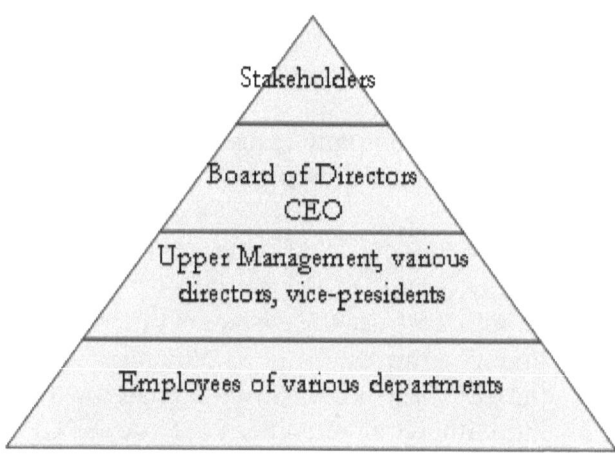

Figure 3.1: Source: Investopedia.com

We generally come across information in newspapers and blogs that talk about CEOs and the BOD and we overlook their purpose or the subtleties that these tidbits of information provide and this leads to make uninformed decisions or opinions. It is important to look at even the slightest details when analysing news about the markets.

We talked about the advantages and disadvantages of corporations and I laid them out cut-and-dry and quite honestly, a little too dry but it is important for you to decide for yourself what the advantages and disadvantages are or for that matter determine if there advantages or disadvantages at all!

In the field of finance there is nothing more benefiting than your opinion, only because it is your own! Therefore, every time you read something within the smooth pages of this book, question every detail of it. If you find errors, which I hope you do not, or if you find something unclear then be sure research it and clear your doubts about it. There is nothing worse than having weak fundamentals that will drag you down later.

The next chapter we will be looking at futures and options, the chapter where we discuss the "future" or at least the relative future. With that thought, let's move onward once more!

Chapter 4

Futures and Options

With this new corporation, Julian could not have been happier. Everything is going exactly as Julian planned and furthermore, is becoming reasonably rich through his invention, the Chorinator. The Chorinator, as you know, is created from various quality parts such as metal which by the way is top quality and is constructed in the finest fashion that being Julian's garage. Nonetheless, the Chorinator is selling and that's all that matters.

From time to time, Julian comes across trouble during the production stages and with the price of the most important component of Chorinator: metal. Every winter it seems that the price of metal decreases and Julian profits increase greatly because with cheap yet quality metal, Julian is able created the same product for less and then sell it for more. Sadly, come summer time, this idea goes in the other direction. During the summer, the price of metal rises and Julian's profits plummet. In Julian's mind, this doesn't make sense and he needs a way out otherwise he will never be able to have a steady, profitable year or even the possibility of one! So, like any good protégé, he contacts his mentor George and explains to him the problem he is having. George in his infinite, mentor-like wisdom explains to Julian to set up a contract between the metal provider and himself with a middle man. He explains the basic premise of the contract, which seems to be very simple. Both of the parties namely, Julian and the metal provider, let's call him Bob, to agree upon a pre-determined price and a delivery date of the product in the future. For example, Julian will promise to buy 1000kg of metal for $10 per pound in June, when he thinks the price of the metal will go up and Bob, promises to sell 1000kg of metal at the same price to Julian because he thinks that is when the price of metal will go down. Now, where does the middle man go? The middle man is responsible for taking the risk/reward of both of the parties. The middle man, will make sure that the price of contract is fulfilled. For example, if the price of the metal decreases to $9 then he will sell to Julian 1000kg of metal for $10 because that is the agreed upon price and will profit $10000. But this can also work in benefit to Julian because if the price of the metal raises to $11 then Julian gets his metal for $10 and the middle man loses $10000.

The contract makes a lot of sense to Julian because he gets a certainty when it comes to buying metal for his Chorinator and Bob, the metal seller gets an assurance that someone will buy his metal at the agreed upon price. Now, that's a win-win.

4.1 Futures

The story of Julian, Bob and the unnamed middle man was a classic example of a **futures contract**.

> Futures contract: A contract between two parties that have the obligation to buy/sell an asset at predetermined date and price.

The futures contract is defined as the obligation to buy/sell a certain asset at a predetermined price and date. The most important bit of information to remember is that a futures contract is an obligation. Therefore, both of the parties *must* fulfil their contracts otherwise, like breaking any contract, consequences can ensue.

A Classic Example

Let's quickly go over the classic example of a wheat farmer and baker; two parties that are essential to each other. The wheat farmer has trouble selling wheat during some times of the season because the price of wheat, for the consumers, is too high. This translates to weak profits or zero profits for the baker because he is unable to produce his bread at a reasonable price and therefore, is unable to sell it. Both parties come to the conclusion that they must set up a futures contract, in order to make some money. Both parties find a middle man/investor that will take the risk of supplying the product at a given date and price and therefore, will also take some of the reward. The wheat farmer and the baker agree that $3/bushel is fair and the baker agrees to buy 1 000 bushels in June. A futures contract is set up between both parties through the investor. If the price of the bushel goes up $1 then the investor is still obligated to provide 1 000 bushels at $3 and is at a loss of $1 000. If the price of the wheat goes down $1 then the investor profits $1 000 because the price of the wheat is now $2 and the baker is obligated to buy it at $3. If you are wondering how the wheat farmer and the baker benefit then the answer is simple, they both get the price that they want. If the price increases then the baker benefits, as he has gotten the wheat cheaper than the market price and vice versa, if the price decreases then the baker loses as he has to buy the wheat at a price that is greater than the market price.

The asset that the futures contract provides is known as the underlying asset therefore, a futures contract is a derivative. Yes, I said it, the dreaded "D word" but not to worry because most derivatives are not complex themselves but it's what you can do with that makes them difficult to understand as a whole.

The underlying asset is what sets the price of futures contract and this is true for all derivatives. As a matter of fact and as a general rule of thumb a derivative is any financial instrument that has an underlying asset and whose price is determined from the underlying asset. For example, options are derivatives because their price is determined by the underlying asset. We will be talking about options in the next section.

It is very important for you to understand right now (1) a futures contract is an *obligation*, something I cannot stress enough and (2) that it is a derivative.

By knowing, these two simple facts, you will be able to understand, relatively quickly other instruments and furthermore, will be able to deal with futures more easily.

Futures and Forwards

A characteristic that all futures have is that they can be traded. If I have set up a futures contract with person A, then I can trade that contract with someone else and gain money for that contract. Thus, a futures contract can be sold like another financial instrument in an exchange unlike a forward. A forward is extremely similar to a future, in that it also has a delivery date, strike price (the price that is agreed upon today), an underlying. The only difference between a Forward and futures is that a Forward *cannot* be traded on an exchange rather a Forward is traded OTC (Over The Counter) meaning the instrument is traded directly between the two concerned parties. Any instrument that is traded between two parties without an exchange is called an OTC trade and by deduction then any instrument traded through an exchange is known as an exchange traded instrument.

Furthermore, forwards are not marked-to-market meaning that the daily ups and downs of the market are not settled on that specific day rather they are settled at the maturity date which differs from a futures contract greatly because futures contract are marked-to market and therefore, require an initial margin, in order to enter into the contract and furthermore, require a maintenance margin to stay in the contract. Mark-to-market is when the ups and downs of the markets are settled then and there. The losses are deducted from your account as they happen and gains are added to your account as they happen. If you do not thoroughly understand this concept right now, not to worry! We will weed out the problems later in the chapter but for now understand that futures are marked-to-market and therefore, require an initial margin and later a maintenance margin.

Since we were on the topic of forwards and futures, I wanted to quickly talk about spot contracts. Spot contracts are like the quick n' dirty futures with a specific difference. Suppose, you wanted the quick delivery of an underlying asset and were willing to settle the date/price now then what could you do? Well, buy a spot contract of course!

By buying a spot contract for an underlying you are essentially deciding to settle "now" or you will be settling in the next couple of days. The date you have decided to settle and are expecting delivery and providing payment is known as the "spot date". This is where the main difference lies between a spot contract and futures or forward contract that the settling is done "now" instead of at a later date.

Futures Market and Constituents

As I mentioned earlier, futures are exchange traded instruments which, as we know, means that an exchange is used to trade between two parties instead of OTC which is, trading without an exchange. Futures contracts can be sold like any other instrument/security that exists. For example, if I wanted to buy a futures contract, I would do the same thing I would do in order to buy a stock/bond which is to contact a broker and have the futures contract bought for a commission. The most "famous" or the most widely known futures exchanges are the NYSE Euronext and the CME Group which allow the futures contracts to be traded.

Futures contracts generally have commodities as their underlying, and it is extremely common to hear "wheat futures" or "corn futures". This is in contrast to an option. An **option** generally has an underlying such as a stock or bond but this can also vary. It is not necessary however, that futures always have commodities as their underlying. A futures contract can have any other security as it underlying, just like an option and as a matter of fact even have intangible things such as interest rates as their underlying.

To side track for a moment, you may ask how is it possible for the underlying to be something intangible. Here the answer is simple. It is very much possible that the futures contract be settled through cash. Therefore, it can also act as a bet.

Getting back on track, futures contracts are very speculative because their price, for one, is determined by the underlying therefore, when the price of the underlying rises, it is high likely so will the price of the futures contract. The more volatile the underlying, the more volatile the futures contract itself. For this reason, futures are widely traded by speculators and hedgers.

Speculation with Futures

Speculators, if you recall, are individuals that are in it for the quick gains and for having a highly leveraged position or in other words having positions that require little margin but the value of the underlying is large. For example, it is possible for you to have a futures contract that has a margin of $10 000 but has underlying assets that are worth more than $100 000. Therefore, the position has been leveraged because for a small amount, you are able to enter into a contract that has underlying that is worth a lot more than the initial amount. The example I have provided is slightly conservative instead it is possible for contracts to have an initial margin of $1 000 and where the underlying of $20 000!

Imagine, yourself walking into the futures exchange with the sudden urge to buy a wheat futures contract because you feel that wheat is doing very well this year. So you buy a wheat Future that is priced at $10 which has an initial margin of $1 000 and there are 100 bushels. Which means that currently your position is worth $10 * 100 = $10 000. After a few days, the price of your futures increases by 50% to $15. Now your position is worth $15 000 because $15 * 100 = $15 000. That's great! With only $1 000 as the initial margin, you were able to gain a tidy sum. Sadly, after a few days, the price of your futures option decreases by $1 and returns back to the original price, which is $10. In this case, you have lost $5 000 and this amount if subtracted from your margin, therefore you owe $4 000! Now imagine, yourself leveraged 30 to 1, meaning for $30 in your position, there is $1 in your margin. Therefore, slight changes in highly leveraged positions can cause a substantial gain or a severe loss.

Hedging Futures

Futures are also used by hedgers – no, not people who cut hedges but people who try to minimize risk in a position.

Before we start hedging with actual futures, we need to thoroughly understand the concept and work with some non-market related items. The best way to think about hedging is to think of it as padding that will minimize the amount of damage (risk) that is being done to your portfolio.

Imagine that you are a football player who has not worn any equipment and therefore, has no padding and are extremely prone to injury (risk). If you get hit by a defensemen you will surely feel the damage as the 200 pound monster takes your frail body and rams it into the ground. At the end of it, you may have a few broken bones and may be in the hospital for quite some time. Now imagine the same situation with equipment. If you take the same hit, you will have effectively minimized the amount of damage due to your "armour" and therefore, you are in the plus or neutral rather than being in the negative without the padding. Hedging is extremely similar to this, except there a lot of variables that you have to watch out for. The padding is what represents the hedging and you represent the position and the 200 pound monster, well that is when the market goes bad, *for you*.

The reason I say "for you" is because not everyone is hoping that the market is going up. Imagine that you have a futures contract that allows you to sell a certain good at a certain price. Then naturally, you would want the price of the good to go down because you want to sell it for the highest price possible and profit from the buyer's loss. For instance, if you have a futures contract that gives you the right and the obligation to sell wheat at $10/bushel and the current price of wheat is at $5/bushel then you have clearly made a profit of $5/bushel even though the market was decreasing. Therefore, as a seller of futures contracts you would want the general trend of the market to be going down. This is known as being short. If, let's say, that we are a buyer of futures contracts, then naturally you want the price of the underlying to increase as much as possible because we have the right and obligation of the seller to sell at the price discussed. This is known as being in a long position. Below I have a graphic which attempts to illustrate short and long.

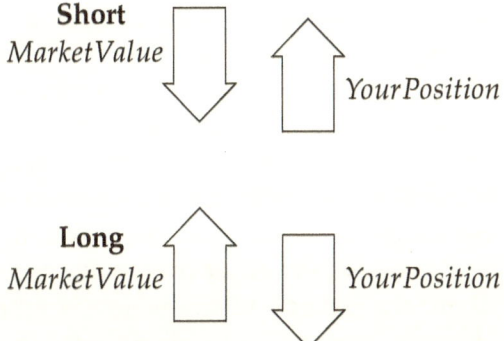

As you can see from the above illustration that either being short or being long is exactly opposite to what the market is and what you want your position to be. To reiterate, being long means you want the market to be up, the left arrow in the figure and your position to be down, in the sense that the contract you have signed allows you to buy, which then translates to buying at a price that is less than market price. Which, once again, means you are benefiting from the spread. To be short, is the exact opposite. You want the market to be down and your position to be up, in the sense that the contract you have signed allows you to sell at a specific price which then translates to you selling at a higher price than the market.

One of the most common questions I get is "why would they want to buy at a price higher than the market price?" Here is where our fundamental understanding of futures come into play. Remember, that a futures gives you the right and the obligation to buy or sell the predetermined underlying at the price it was decided beforehand. Therefore, the buyer is obligated to buy from you even if the price is lower in the market and the seller is obligated to sell to you even if the price is higher in the market.

We can now talk about hedging with futures. Hedging with futures contracts has to, primarily, do with trying to minimize the risk of your position by "locking" in a price of the underlying in the present, in hopes that it will increase or decrease in the future, depending on your position.

If you recall earlier in the chapter, we talked about the baker and the wheat farmer and how they essentially wanted to minimize their risk and continue to make profits or at least, in some shape or form, have a precise level of certainty. Unbeknownst to you, they were actually hedging their position.

For example, imagine that you are a baker and in the future, you will be buying 100 bushels of wheat in order to make flour for your bread and pastries. Currently, the price of wheat is $5/bushel but a current futures contract offers a price of $4/bushel in July. Therefore, if you buy the futures contract, you have "hedged" against a risk that might occur in the future. Suppose, the price of wheat increases to $6 in July, then you have successfully hedged your position by buying at only $4/bushel and there-fore, maintaining your profit margin. Suppose, if you had not bought the futures contract, then you would have to settle for $6/bushel and your profits would decrease.

However, hedging has its drawbacks after all, there is no such thing as a free lunch. Imagine that you bought the futures contract but come July, the price of the wheat is $3/bushel! Then you will be at a loss because you are now obligated to buy wheat for $4 when in reality you could have been buying for only $3. If your hunch or your research does not work out then you could be suffering a loss from the hedge itself, which would indeed be ironic.

Hedging becomes extremely prevalent when options are used, primarily because you could use options to offset the losses of stocks or bonds or pretty much anything that you could bet on. Fur-thermore, hedging is a difficult topic to understand thoroughly because of the various perspectives it provides. When hedging your position or your portfolio, not only do you have to pay attention to the hedge but also to the underlying and fur-thermore, to the financial instrument that is being hedged. In addition, to those variables, you have to also be weary of the fact that the hedge may turn around and could cost your expected loss and more. Therefore, hedging is a complicated task and fur-thermore, is difficult to handle once a magnitude of variables are introduced into the equation.

Margin

There is no relationship between margin and ticks but it is quite important to talk about these topics since these are the only topics that have not yet been approached.

We talked earlier about margin and did not dive too much into the topic but now is the time to do so. We said earlier that there were two types of margin, firstly initial margin and then maintenance margin. The primary purpose of having these is because of the fact that futures are mark to market, as opposed to other financial instruments such as a stocks.

Having a financial instrument that is trade mark to market means that the daily ups and downs of the market are dealt with then and there. For example, if I had a futures contract that lost money on an arbitrary date then the losses of that day would be accounted for and would be subtracted from my account or my maintenance margin. Similarly, if I gained money from my contract then that amount would be added to my account. As I mentioned earlier, futures are not like forwards, where the money is settled at a later date, futures are settled *then* and *there*.

With that in mind, having an initial margin and a maintenance margin is extremely important. Without these, transactions cannot take place. Recall, that the initial margin is the margin that is required to enter a position and a maintenance margin is the margin that is required to stay in the position. Therefore, when the positive/negative fluctuations of the market occur, the money gained/lost is taken from the maintenance margin. Suppose, that in a leveraged position or even in a position that is constantly losing, we come to the point where the money lost is less than the maintenance margin. Then what would happen? Since, it is mandatory for you to stay within your maintenance margin, your broker will do a **margin call**, a term that you may have heard before and you will be required to refill the margin up to the initial margin. For instance, I have a futures contract that requires me to have an initial margin of $2 000 and a maintenance margin of $1 000. Due to a turbulent market, consecutive losses occur and my maintenance margin falls below $1 000 to say $800 then my broker will do a margin call and inform me that I have to refill the account right now. So I will transfer $1 200 to my account to refill my maintenance margin to the initial margin which is $2 000.

In the event, that I do not refill my account, the brokerage firm will liquidate my account or in other words, sell my position and recover from any losses that may have occurred.

Leverage and Margin

As you know, leverage and margin go hand in hand. If your contract is leveraged and encounters a small change in price then in one hit, you could be out of your maintenance margin and would be required to refill it. The problem lies in refilling the margin. Imagine that you are in a position where you were required to pay a maintenance margin of $1 000 and an initial margin of $2 000. The contract is leveraged 10 : 1 meaning, for every $1 you have in your margin, you will have $10 in your position. Hence, if you lose $1 in your position, you will be required to pay $10 from your margin. Imagine this scaled up to the hundreds of dollars. Then, if you lose $100 in your position, you will be required to pay $1 000! In just one shot, you have lost all of your maintenance margin and will be required to refill it to the initial margin. If you do not have the money to refill the account then your position will be liquidated but that is not necessarily the case if you are the broker-age firm. Take the perspective of a institution that invests in various contracts which are leveraged. Within their portfolio, they have over 50 contracts that are highly leveraged. If 10 of the positions crumble, they will be required to pay a hefty sum. In the event that they do not have that money, they will be required to file for bankruptcy! Therefore, highly leveraged positions and low margins can be very risky if precautions are not taken.

In essence, the important thing to understand is that since futures are mark-to-market, it is required for you to have a margin. Therefore, you can assume that any financial security that is mark to market will have some sort of margin that will be required to enter the position and to stay in the position.

Tick, Tick, Tick

Like all markets that exist around the world, futures markets move in their price, obviously. But what is not obvious is the fact that futures markets have what is known as a "tick" and I don't mean the small arachnids that are on your dog and annoy the hell out of it but rather a tick that requires a minimum fluctuation in price, upwards or downwards if there is to be one. This is known, more concretely as the **tick size**.

> Tick size: The minimum price fluctuation, up or down, of a futures market.

For example, a futures market may have a tick size of 0.10. Therefore, the market itself has to move that amount even if the amount is less than the actual movement. Let me clarify further. Suppose, the market moved 0.01 and the tick size was 0.10 then the market would automatically have to move the extra 0.09 in order to maintain the tick size. This is true for all futures markets, take for example the Canadian Dollar Futures market (remember, that the underlying of a futures contract could be practically anything). The CAD futures market has a tick size of 0.0001 (cmegroup.com). Therefore, the minimum amount the market could move or has to move if there is movement is 0.0001.

The tick sizes I have shown are unit-less but that is not always true because there are markets where the tick size is a dollar value such as $0.025 or even $0.005. Therefore, the tick size can be either unit-less or have a dollar value assigned.

Do not however that the tick size is not the amount that affects a futures contract directly. Rather, the tick size is merely the amount the market has to move if it *does* move. What does effect a futures contract directly, in some sense, is the **tick value**.

> Tick Value: The minimum dollar fluctuation in relation to the tick size.

For instance, the tick value of CAD futures market is $10.0 (cmegroup.com) meaning that for every 0.0001 change in the market, we can expect to see a $10.00 profit or loss in the contract. Thus, the profit or loss of $10.00 is added or subtracted from your account. Remember, it is not necessary for the market to shift in only multiples of the tick size, it can change by a number that is not a multiple of the tick size in which case, the amount subtracted or added is the one that is the nearest to a multiple of the tick size. Let's say the market shifts by 0.006 when the tick size is 0.005 and the tick value is $10.00 then the amount added or subtracted will be $0.006/0.005 multiplied by the tick value.

The most important aspect to understand about ticks is the fact that all futures markets have predetermined tick sizes and tick values. To reiterate, the tick size is the minimum amount the market has to move if it does move and the tick value is the dollar value of the movement that occurs. It is as simple as that.

Finishing Up Futures

If there is anything that you have picked up in the past fourteen odd pages then it should be that a futures is a right and an obligation to deliver some underlying good at a predetermined date. That, in my opinion, is the most important thing to understand. More often than not, I find myself talking to people who know things but they do not understand them – there's a difference. When you truly understand a concept, you can twist, turn it, cut it, you can do anything with it because you understand the basis of the argument or the logical reasoning behind it.

That's what is important to understand, the fundamentals behind a concept otherwise, applying imagination will be extremely difficult.

Recap

Let's quickly recap futures and move onto its more celebrated cousin: the option.

Starting from the top, we talked about the futures, once again, as an instrument that gives us the right and the obligation to buy or sell a good at a specific date in the future. The contract is set-up by an investor who is willing to take some of the risk and therefore, some of the reward in order to set up the contract. The predetermined date is commonly known as the delivery date and the price that is agreed upon for the underlying, which is the good that is to be traded, is known as the strike price.

The unique thing about the futures contract is, as opposed to the Forward contract, is the fact that it is not OTC or the fact that it is not traded on an exchange. Furthermore, what else sets the futures contract apart from the Forward contract is the fact that it is mark-to-market meaning that the ups and downs of the market are accounted for as they happened, as opposed to the forward contract. Therefore, some sort of margin is needed to add and subtract the gains/losses. The amount needed to enter into a futures contract is known as an initial margin and the margin that is needed to stay in the position is known as the maintenance margin. If the account goes below the maintenance margin then a margin call is issued by the broker which requires you to replenish your account. In the event that you cannot replenish your account then you position will be liquidated in order to recover from the losses that may have occurred.

There are two parties that commonly trade a futures contract: these are either speculators or hedgers. Recall, that a speculator is someone who is looking for a "quick buck" from volatile positions in the market and a hedger is someone who is trying to "pad" their position against any unwanted risk. These hedgers or speculators could be either long or short. If a position is long then the investor is looking for the market to go up and if the investor is short then they are looking for the market to be down.

Overall, the futures contract is a great way to maintain some level of certainty in an uncertain world with the risk that you may lose some amount of money or by the same token, may gain some money.

4.2 Options

Finally, we are on to the options contract or simply the option, the more complicated,in terms of understanding and easily misunderstood cousin of the futures contract. The Option differs greatly from the futures contract both at its core and otherwise. This portion of the chapter will contain various terms about the Option and furthermore, will contain some concepts that are associated with the instrument. Without further delay, let's move onward.

Option Basics

The option is an interesting instrument because it allows the investor to be extremely imaginative with it. Unlike a futures contract where you the right and the obligation to buy or sell, in an option contract, you only have the right and not the obligation to exercise the option. This is the most important thing to understand about options, that fact that the owner of the option has the right but not the obligation to exercise their option.

> Option: The right but not the obligation
> to buy or sell the underlying asset.

Since, we have not dived into option terminology, I will go into an example that involves options themselves rather I'll try to make an analogy that best fits the situation. Suppose, you are interested in a buying a car. You go to the dealership and you pick out your car and you ask for the price tag. The salesperson tells you that the price of the car is $20000. You think to yourself "That's a lot of money, I should think this one over." So you ask the salesperson if they could give you some sort of guarantee that the car you love won't be bought by someone else in other words, you are asking them if they are willing to give you the right to buy the car but not the obligation. The salesperson agrees for a price to write the contract which states you have the right and not the obligation to buy the car before a predetermined date. In the event, that you don't buy the car, all you lose is the money you spent on the contract. So you agree with the salesperson and pay him, let's say, $100 for the right to the buy the car before July. The price of the contract would have differed, if you had chosen a different car. July comes by and you decide "sure, why the heck not? I'll buy the car" and so you buy the car and that's that.

The moral of the story is the fact that you signed a contract that gave you the right and not the obligation to buy the car in exchange for $100. In the event that you don't buy the car, the only thing that you have lost is the $100 that you paid to buy the contract and this is no big deal because even if did buy the car, you weren't going to get the money back. Therefore, the money is not to be confused with a deposit.

Thus, the contract is analogous to an options contract and the car is analogous to the underlying of the Option. Note, that I have stated that the Option has an underlying and the price of the Option is dependent on the underlying. Therefore, if you recall from the futures section, an options contract is a derivative.

If we continue with the analogy of the car then we can say that our contract would have been more expensive if the car was more expensive or had a different characteristic attached to it. Therefore, instead of costing you $100 to gain the contract, it could have cost you $200 or even more. Thus, the price of an option is dependent on the price of the underlying among other factors which will we talk about later in the chapter.

Right into Terminology

In the story we briefly talk about an arbitrary date before which we have to make our decision otherwise, the contract becomes useless. In option terms this is known as the **expiration date**. The expiration date is the date at which the option contract is valid after this date the contract is null and void. The expiration date differs from the delivery date because before the delivery date, the holder of the future contract cannot get the underlying. This, however, is not the case for an options contract. The options can be **exercised** before the expiration date. When I talk about exercising an option, I am essentially talking about using the option.

When an option contract is bought, the price at which the underlying is to be bought or sold before a predetermined date is known as the **strike price**. Imagine that you had an option contract that allowed you to buy ABC stock at $50 before July then the strike price of that contract would be $50.

The price of the option itself is known as the **premium** of option and is dependent on various factors such as the expiration date, the strike price, the current price of the underlying and the predicted volatility. Options are priced using the Black-Scholes formula, something we won't go into but the basis of the formula are those factors that I mentioned earlier.

On the next page I have an image how options are framed so that they provide enough information to the buyer to help him/her understand what he/she is getting into. Ignore the word "call" in this scenario as it is not important right now.

The illustration I have shown above shows how traders will convey their message to other traders about the option that they are selling. As shown, in the diagram, ABC represents the underlying asset.

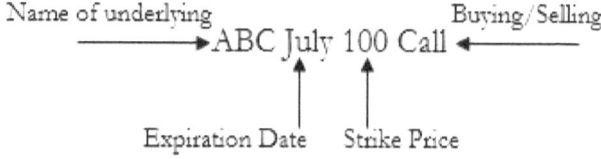

Generally, this asset is a stock but that is not always true. Recall from the futures section that derivatives can practically have anything as their underlying. Working from left to right, you'll notice that there is a month. As indicated by the diagram, that is the expiration date. Though, it does not offer a specific day, the expiration is generally on the third Friday of the month in question (investopedia.com). Therefore, the expiration date for our option will be on the third Friday of July. Next on our list is the strike price. As we discussed earlier, the strike price is the price at which the underlying can be bought or sold, in this case it is bought because it is a call option. Therefore, if the option is exercised, the cost of ABC will be $100 per share. Note, that every option contract contains 100 shares of the underlying if the underlying happens to be stock. Throughout, this portion of the chapter, you can assume that we will be referring to options that have stock as their underlying.

Writers and Holders

There are terms for everything in the markets, as you just saw to exercise an option is to use it or to redeem it. You have probably already guessed from my title that there are terms for people who buy options and for people who sell options. Those who buy options are known as holders and those who sell options are known as writers. Like I said, writers don't write much and holders don't hold much other than the fact they either buy or sell an option respectively. These terms will come in use when we talk about puts and calls. Therefore, it essential that you understand that holders are people who buy options and writers are people who sell options.

A Buyer's Perspective on Calls and Puts

The basis of most confusion when talking about options is the misunderstanding or the lack of understanding of the terms "call" and "put". More often than not, the two are confused and are further confused when talking about buying/selling calls and buying/selling puts. Therefore, we will be spending quite some time on the idea of a "call" and "put". The primary reason, I did not include the notion of selling calls is because at this point the concept could get a little confusing. So for now, we will take the perspective of the buyer and then move into the perspective of the seller.

Additionally, I encourage you to keep a pencil and paper handy for this portion to write draw some diagrams to illustrate your understanding to yourself or to just take notes. Try your best to understand the core of the idea and if you can do that successfully then you have nothing to worry about.

The Call

Let's get started with a "call" because those are slightly easier to understand than puts.

Call: From a buyers' perspective, a call allows them to buy the underlying at the strike price. Holders are known to have a long position and writers are known to have a short position.

Let's dive into a quick example to settle the definition. Say for example, you bought a July call option that had a strike price of $50 for the ABC company. This could alternatively be written as "ABC July $50 Call". This essentially means, you have bought the right but not the obligation to buy 100 ABC stock for $50 before the third Friday of July. Let's say you decide to exercise your call option then you will be required to pay $50000 because there are 100 shares that your call option requires you to buy for the strike price which is $50. Consequently, the total amount comes $50000 because $50 * 100.

Fairly simple to understand right? I find that the main confusion comes from trying to understand exactly how a holder will benefit from having a call or a put something we will be discussing next. The idea is slightly unintuitive, in my opinion and therefore, is confused by people who try to understand. So, for the time being try to not let your intuitive side get the better of you.

Let's recap exactly what a call option does. A call option allows the holder to buy the underlying for a specific strike price. Furthermore, the holder has the right to buy the underlying but not the obligation to do so because he/she is holder and not a writer, something we have to pay attention too.

The primary question that arises is "how does the holder benefit?" In order to benefit from a call option, the price of the underlying has to go up, so you can buy it for cheaper and profit from the difference between the current market value and the price you paid for the stock. Take for example an ABC June $10 call that gives you the right to buy 100 ABC shares for $10 before the third Friday of June. The only way you can benefit from the option is if the price of ABC increases above $10 to say $11 otherwise the option is worthless. Why must the market price increase above the strike price, you ask? Since, the call option gives the right to buy the stock, therefore, if we buy the stock for $10 then we can acquire 100 shares for $10 and then resell them for $11 each. Therefore, profiting $1 per share. Not too bad right? The higher the price of the underlying, the better for the holder of a call option. Holders of call options benefit from market increases and lose when the market for the underlying is below that of the strike price. Imagine, that the price of the underlying was $9 and the strike price for your option was $10 then would you want to buy the underlying for $1 higher than the market price? Of course not! On the next page is a diagram to help you visualize why call option holders benefit from the market price of the underlying being higher than that of the strike price.

This may be a slightly confusing diagram at first but I will clear up any confusions that you may have. The market price, I have indicated as a circle with an "x", and it is a point because it can fluctuate. The strike price is a line because it remains constant until and up to the expiration date. The holder can

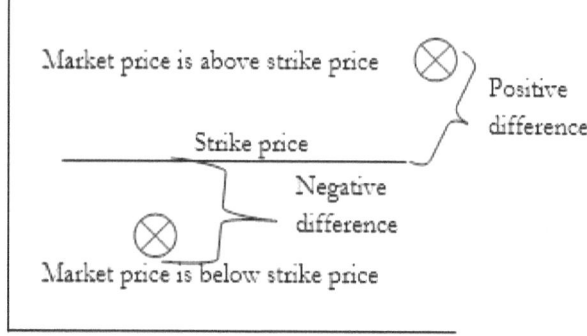

Figure 4.1: Shows the relationship between the strike price and the market price.

only benefit if the circle is above the line because he/she wants buy the underlying for less and then sell it for more. If the market price is below the strike price, as indicated by a circle in the diagram then there is no use in buying the underlying, which is more than the current market price and then trying to sell it because not everyone will buy it. It will be extremely difficult to turn a profit in that situation. In order for a call holder to benefit, the market price of the underlying has to be above the strike price. Let's take another example, so the idea is cemented into your mind. Suppose you had a BCA January $50 call then this means that the expiration date is on the third Friday of January, the strike price is $50 and it is a call option. The price of the underlying, which is BCA, has to be above $50 in order for us to profit. Suppose, the market price of BCA increases to $55 and you decide this is a good time to exercise your option so you do. So, you buy 100 BCA for $50 a piece which costs your $50 000 and you sell them for $55 which leads to a profit of $5 per share for every share that you hold! In essence you made $55 000 − $50 000 = $5 000 from which you have to subtract the amount of money you paid for the option itself but nonetheless, $5 000 is a pretty hefty sum. Suppose, the market price for BCA dropped to $45 then it would be useless for you to exercise your option and thus, you will only lose the amount you paid for the option.

In, Out and At

There only three things that can happen when you are holding a call option (and a put option but the definitions change). One, the call option is "in-the-money" meaning the market price is above the strike price. You can think of it as, being full of money because the market price is above the strike price. Therefore, in-the-money call options are when the market price is above the strike price. There are call options that are also known as "deep in-the-money" call options meaning the difference between the market price and the strike price is large. Take for example an ABC July $30 call. Suppose, the market price of ABC is $60 then the option is considered to be "deep in-the-money".

Two, the call option is "out-of-the-money" meaning that market price is below the strike price.

Three, the call option is "at-the-money" meaning that the strike price and market price are equal. Understand that currently we are talking about buying call options. Once we switch to put, the meaning of the terms change. Thus, it is important to understand the difference in both call and put and furthermore, understand we are talking from the buyers' perspective.

The Put

Let's move onto puts from a buyers' perspective. Meaning, we are the ones that will be buying **put** options.

> Put: From a buyers' perspective, the right and not the obligation to sell the underlying for the strike price before the expiration date.

Take for example an ADC July $30 put which gives the right and not the obligation to sell the underlying, in this case ADC, at the $30 a piece. For instance, suppose you have the same put option and the current market price for ADC is $45. You have a put option that allows you to sell ADC for $30 but currently that option is worthless because the market price is higher than that of the strike price. Think of a put option as the opposite of a call option. In essence, call options will benefit if the market price is above the strike price and put options will not benefit if the market price is above the strike price.

If, in our scenario, the market price is below that of the strike price then we benefit because we are able to sell the underlying for a price that is higher than the current market price and therefore, benefit from the difference between the market price and the strike price. Suppose, our ADC July $30 put was in-the-money, meaning that strike price was above the market price and the market price for ADC was

$20. Seeing as how we make $10 per share, we decide to exercise the option and sell 100 at $30 which the writer of the put is obligated to buy. This means we have made $10 per share ($10 * 100 = $10000) from which we have to subtract the cost of the option itself.

If our put option was out-of-the-money, then we can assume the option itself was worthless for the time being if the expiration was far away or completely worthless if it remained the same, until expiration date. This is because an out-of-the-money put option has the strike price below the market price. Here's a quick diagram to help you understand put options.

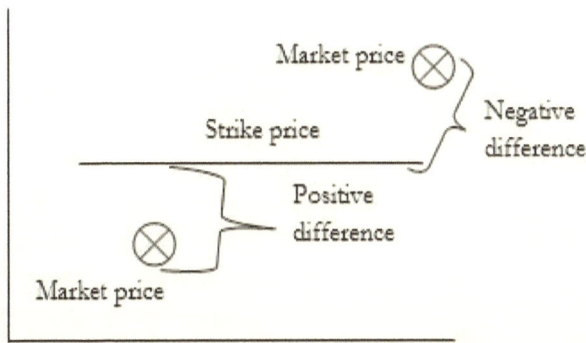

Figure 4.2: Shows the relationship between the strike price of a put and the market price. Notice the "oppositeness" from a call.

The diagram explains how it is beneficial to have the market price below the strike price and not beneficial to have the market price of the above the strike price.

If you refer back to the diagram, you will notice that the difference between the strike price and the market price, when the market price is below the strike price, is positive because we have the right to sell the underlying at a price that is higher than that of market price. In the event, that market price is above the strike price then we are at a loss because we can sell the underlying for a profit, but not necessarily because we have to account for the price of the option itself.

Therefore, in-the-money put options are options when the strike price is above the market price and out-of-the-money put options are options that have the strike price below the market price. This is the exact opposite of an in-the-money and out-of-money call option. If you recall, we said that out-of-the-money call options were options whose strike price was above the market price and in-the-money call options were options whose strike price was below the market price.

This may sound very confusing at first but once you understand the logic behind it, it will make intuitive sense. A call option gives the holder the ability to *buy* the underlying at the strike price. Would you want to buy something for more than it is worth on the market? No, of course not. You want it for the cheapest price possible. Therefore, if you have the right to buy something, you are hoping that what you are buying is significantly below the market price. Assume, you had a call option that allowed you to buy apples for a $10. The current price of the apples was $20. Then, this would be a great time to exercise your option because you can buy the apples for much cheaper than they are right now in the market. Suppose, the price of those apples was $9 and you had the right and not obligation to buy them for $10, would you? Of course not! Why pay more, when you can pay less? Therefore, we can say that option for apples is in-the- money when the market price is above the strike price and out-of-the-money when the strike price is market price is below the strike price.

Let's consider a similar analogy with a put option. Note, that a put option gives the holder the right and not the obligation to sell the underlying at the strike price. Say, for example, you had 100 apples and you bought a put option that gave you the right and not the obligation to sell those apples to the writer for a strike price which in this case is $10. Again, would you want to sell your apples for less than the market price, which is $15? No, of course not! You want to get the prime amount for your apples. Therefore, you want to sell the apples when they are above the market price. Imagine, if the market price for the apples drops to $8 and you have the right to sell the apples for $10 then why not? You get to make $2 per apple for 100 apples. Therefore, you would say that you are in-the-money, for a put option, when the strike price is above the market price and out-of-the-money when the strike price is below the market price.

Again, the most important aspect of this scenario is to understand the fact that holding a put option gives you the ability to sell the underlying for the strike price and holding a call option gives you the ability to buy the underlying for the strike price.

Before we move on to the sellers' perspective of calls and puts, I would like you to take your pencil/pen and your paper and write down all the various things you can do with calls and puts. Think about, how you can speculate with them and how you can hedge with them since these are the most important aspects of option trading.

From the Sellers' Perspective: Calls and Puts

Calls and Puts change drastically in their fundamentals and their workings when we deal with the sellers' perspective. The primary reason is because we are required to dive deeper into the meaning of both the words and furthermore, understand thoroughly the nature of options.

At the beginning of the chapter, we defined options as the right and not the obligation of a buyer/seller to buy or sell the underlying at the strike price before the expiration date. What requires emphasis is the fact that we *bought* the right instead of selling the right. Since, we bought the right we do not have an obligation, like we said when we defined an option but if we sold the right then we do have an obligation. Let me explain further. If I give you the right to sell something to me, then I have the obligation to buy that something from you, in case you choose to exercise your right. Thus, lies the crux of the perspective. The fact that the writer is obligated to buy or sell, if the holder wishes to execute their option.

In addition, I would like to add the fact that writing options is riskier than holding them because in this situation you are bonded by the contract, in the event that they choose to exercise their right.

Therefore, you cannot "get away" from a trade. For example, if you are holding a call option then you can choose to exercise the option or not but with writing the option, you do not have that sort of liberty. If the holder chooses to exercise their option then you must oblige. Therefore, making the proposition risky.

Let's try and work an example where we are selling a call option or in other words are writing a call option. Recall, that a call option gives the holder the right and not the obligation to buy the underlying for a certain strike price. If we write a call, we are giving the holder the right to buy the underlying from us and furthermore, we are obligated to sell them the underlying if they choose to exercise their call. Suppose, that you are writing an ABC July $30 call that gives the holder the right to 100 shares of ABC for $30 per share. For this contract, you will charge a $1 premium meaning you are charging them $1 for every share for the contract. Thus, the contract costs $100.

If you merely look at the macro, you have gained $100 in the event that the holder does not exercise their option and in the event that the option is in-the-money for the buyer, you have lost some amount by selling to them 100 shares of ABC for $30. The macro is simple enough to understand and for the most part, the only thing that matters.

Let's first deal with the scenario that will make money for us when the option is out-of-the-money for the holder. If the option is out-of-the-money then from the holders' perspective, the strike price is above the market price. In this case, we have benefited because the holder will not exercise their option and we will gain the premium which is 100.

In the case, that holder does exercise their option, then the issue is a little different. Suppose, the market price for the ABC is $40 on the third Friday of July then in the situation the holder will, of course, exercise their option because they get to buy ABC for $30. So you have to provide them with ABC for $30, where you lose $10 per share, which you could have gained. Therefore, you lost $30 * 100 - $100 = $2\,900$ because $100 was gained as the premium for contract itself. Providing the holder with the underlying when you already have underlying known as a covered call. A covered call, essentially means that you have the underlying at your disposal beforehand and have no problem providing underlying. Now, the natural questions arises "can you have options that are not covered?" Well, I think you know the answer.

If you are writing a call option where you do not have the underlying, that is known as a writing a naked call. Which, as I stated earlier means, that you do not have the underlying and will buy the underlying if the holder chooses to exercise their option. There are various risks that are associated with this and you can figure out why. Imagine that the price of the underlying tripled from $20 to $60 and you had to provide 100 shares of that stock for a mere $20 then you are in deep doo-doo because you will have to buy 100 shares for $60 which is $6000 and then sell them for $2\,000$, that's a $4\,000$ loss! That is why, before writers write naked calls, they are required by their brokers to provide a level of equity, kind of like a margin in case the worst happens. Naked calls are extremely risky, as you can tell therefore, only experts deal with them.

Quick Recap

Let's a do a quick recap of writing calls. Writing a call, gives the holder the right to buy the underlying from you at the strike price and gives you the obligation to provide them with the underlying if the right is exercised. The writer of a call option has two possibilities underneath his sleeve. The first possibility, where he gains money, is if the call option he writes for a premium is not exercised by the holder and thus, the writer gains the amount that is the premium.

Recall, that the premium of any contract is some x multiplied by 100 shares because that is how many shares come in every options contract. There is one thing to note, however. In the scenarios, we currently dealing with, we are using American style options, yes there are various types of options that exist. For example, there are European style options that can only can be exercised at the expiration date. Which is completely different from American style options because they can be exercised at any time during their lifetimes.

The other possibility is when the writer of the call option loses. In the event, that call option is in-the-money for the holder then he will surely exercise it. Upon exercising the option, the writer has to provide the holder with the 100 shares of the underlying for the strike price which we already have in our portfolio. This, we said, was known as a covered call. As stated earlier, it is very possible that the writer has written a naked call option, which means that the writer does not have the underlying at his disposal. In the event that the holder exercises the call option, the writer will immediately have to buy the underlying for whatever price it is and provide it to the holder. This, we said, was extremely risky because the price of the underlying could have increased substantially which meant that we would have to buy the shares for a higher price than before.

In essence, what you have to know about writing calls is that you are giving the holder the right, over "your" shares for a premium and furthermore, are giving up the liberty or gaining the obligation to provide the holder with 100 shares of the underlying.

Writing a Put

Writing puts is slightly confusing but it is nothing that we cannot handle. Recall, that a put is essentially giving the holder the right to sell the underlying to the writer. When you write puts, you are giving the holder the right to sell you the underlying for the strike price and you are providing this obligation, which you have, at a premium.

Let's cut to the chase. Suppose, you are writing an ABC Jan $30 put or in other words, you are giving the holder of this option the right to sell ABC to you for $30. Just as we did for the call option, let's talk about where the writer of a put option can make money. When the put option is out-of-the-money, the writer will make the premium that he/she has charged. An out-of-the-money put option, is an option whose strike price is below the market price. Therefore, the holder will not exercise the option because he/she does not want to sell the underlying for a price that is below the market price. In this scenario the writer will make the premium. Suppose we wrote a put option with a premium of $100 or $1 per share. The price of ABC turned in our favour and increased above the strike price to $35 so the holder did not exercise their option and therefore, we gained the premium which was $100.

If, however, the price of the underlying did not turn in our favour and moved below the strike price to $25 which means the put option is in-the-money. This time the holder will exercise his right because he can sell you the underlying for $30 and since you have sold that right to him, you are obligated to buy it from him. Therefore, you lose $5 for every share that you buy or $500 total for 100 shares.

When the put option is in-the-money (ITM) it is bad for us and when the option is out-of-the-money (OTM), the situation is good for us because the holder will not exercise their option and therefore, we can gain the premium. Writing puts is relatively simple once you understand the general concept behind them. They are just like calls but the opposite.

For the curious reader, I would like to mention that are such as things are covered puts and naked puts but we will not being going to the meaning of these types of puts.

In essence, what you have to understand when you are writing puts is that you are giving the holder of the put the ability to call upon you at any time to buy his/her shares. Therefore, you have the obligation to buy the shares, if holder says so. The rest of details, you can extract and deduce from prior knowledge.

Understanding, the fundamentals of the markets and anything in general is the key to understanding the whole of the topic. More often than not, I come across people who have only scratched the surface of a topic and use complicated words to show people around them what they "know" but in reality, it is not much because if I were to ask them to become creative and imaginative with their understanding or their knowledge then it would prove to be difficult for them. Therefore, I should emphasize, strongly, that when you are going through various topics within the confines of this book try to understand, thoroughly, the fundamentals of the topic.

Hedging and Speculating

Just as futures can be hedged and speculate so can options but options even more so. The primary reasons why anyone ever buys options is because they would like to either hedge their position or speculate their position in order to earn a "quick buck".

Hedging with options can get quite complicated because we run into the "Greeks", which are various variables that provide information about the option and the underlying such as a **delta**, **vega**, **gamma** and **theta**. We will not be diving into the Greeks thoroughly because that is not the scope of the book but I will give you a brief description of each, so you at least have a basic understanding of them and more importantly, so you don't look dumbfounded when someone says "what's the delta?"

The Delta and Gamma

Let's address the question since it was asked. The delta of an option shows the movement ratio between the price of underlying and the price of the option. Therefore, if you have an option that had a delta of 0.5 then for every $1 change in the underlying, you can expect that the price of the option will change by $0.5. When options are in-the-money they approach a value of 1 When the expiration date is approaching and out-of-the-money options approach −1 when they are close to the expiration date. This is fairly logically because if there is an ITM option that is nearing expiration and it remains ITM then the price of option will rise along and movement will become synchronous or in other words, for everyone $1 change in the underlying, there will be a $1 change in the price of the option. The opposite is true for OTM options where for every $1 change in the underlying, the price of option will decrease by $1. To reiterate, ITM options near expiry work in tandem, with every $1 increment in the underlying, there is a $1 increment in the option and OTM options near expiry will lose $1 for every $1 gain in the underlying. When talking about delta, we must talk about its (mathematical) first derivative which is gamma.

In essence, the gamma of an option is the "slope" or the rate of change of the delta in comparison to the price of the underlying asset. On the next page, I have a graph that demonstrates the slope of a delta is the gamma.

The graph shows that the gamma is the slope of a delta graph which is the relationship between the price of the underlying and the price of the option.

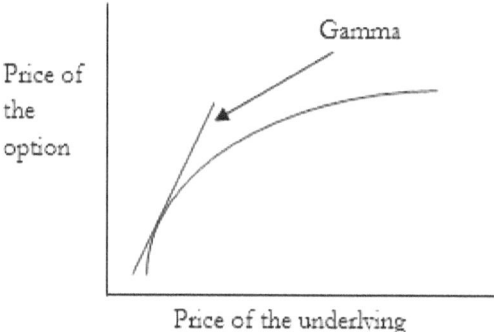

I promised there would not be a lot of math but it is required. If you wish, you can just skip to the next section which does not contain math.

The gamma shows the relationship between delta and the price of the underlying asset. If have you taken calculus or even pre-calculus then you understand that the gamma will be different at all points on the graphs by even the smallest decimal value. Though the graph, does not show any values, gamma is the largest when the option is ATM (at-the-money) and the smallest when the gamma is ITM or OTM. Therefore, the gamma will attempt to show you how much the option will be ITM or OTM depending on the price of the underlying. If you are confused with this concept, not to worry, we will not be dealing with this after. However, it still important for you to know and understand the importance of gamma and delta.

Vega and Theta

Moving on we encounter the vega and the theta both which are not related but seem to be in pairs all the time.

To put simply, the vega of an option is the relationship between the price and the 1% change in volatility of the underlying asset. In essence, 3 of the 4, Greeks show the relationship between an aspect of the option and an aspect of the underlying asset. In the case for vega, it happens to be the relationship between the price of the option and the 1% volatility of the underlying asset. As you know, the volatility of an asset is the measure of the price fluctuation of security over time. In other words, volatility measures how quickly or how slowly the price of an asset can move. You will see a high vega if the volatility of the asset is low and vice versa, you will see a low vega if the volatility of the asset is high. Furthermore, the vega moves to zero as the expiration for the option nears.

At last, we have theta which in my opinion is the easiest understand out of all the Greeks. In essence, Theta tells us how much money the option will lose depending on its strike price over time. Therefore, it shows the decreasing time value of the option assuming that all variables remain constant throughout the period of the option. For example, suppose you had an option that had a strike price of $100 and its Theta was 10 then you can say that every day the price of the option will drop by 10 until expiry assuming that all of the other variables remain constant.

Wrapping up the Greeks

There you have it, "the Greeks", ladies and gentleman. You could use the Greeks for various things in option trading and they are great way to understand, exactly how you option is doing. Now, we can finally talk about hedging using an option.

Recall, when we are hedging we want to minimize the damage our portfolio takes in the event that parts of the portfolio take a dive for the worse.

The basic principle in option hedging is to offset loss through a call option or a put option. In this scenario we will be dealing with a put option. Suppose, you had a portfolio that had various stocks and bonds that were matched just right – in your opinion. The markets are doing well, in your opinion, so you decide to buy 100 shares of ABC corp. for $20 a piece, bringing the grand total to $2 000. Even though you are confident in your trade, you still want to mitigate any risk that might occur. So you buy a put option for ACB, another stock that you own, for $100 which gives you the ability to sell ACB for $25 apiece before June.

What you aim to do with put is too offset the loss of ABC with the gain you make from exercising the ACB put that you own. Suppose, that your hunch for ABC is false and the stock takes a dive to $15. That means you just lost $500 and this is a hit that you can't take. Luckily, your put option is ITM. So you decide to offset the loss by exercising your put option which allows you to sell your ACB which you bought for $20, for $25! Therefore, making a $500 profit. So, you exercise your put option and gain $500 but with the previous loss of $500 from ABC, the net loss/gain is $100 rather than the original $600 (assuming the put did not work out). Why $100 you ask and why not zero? Well, that is because you paid $100 for the put option. Therefore, being $100 in loss but the upside of arrangement is that you are not at a loss of $600.

This the basic premise behind hedging using options. Basically, you want to utilize a call or a put and try to offset any loss that you may think might occur. Of course, actually hedging using options get more complicated once you implement the Greeks.

Speculation

As you know, options are often used as a tool of speculation. Speculation, as you know, is when make risky investments, which are essentially bets, in order to make money. Options are quite frequently used to speculate because they provide a wide variety of possibilities. Not only can you speculate that a security is going to go up but you can also speculate that the security will go down.

For example, you can be a holder that is hoping that the market price is greater than the strike price, so you can exercise your option or you can be the writer of the option and hope that the strike price greater than the market price. In either scenario, one party is betting against the other to fail.

Wrapping Up

The wonders of options cannot be explained within a section of a book but I have tried to do so nonetheless. We talked about options as the right and not the obligation for the buyer/seller to buy or sell the underlying. Options provide a great alternative to experienced investors that want to develop new strategies in order to profit. In my opinion, options are one of few securities out there that allow for so much creativity and imagination when it comes to portfolio management. Furthermore, the ability of the option to be so versatile also sets it apart from the various securities that exist in the markets. One can think of an option as the more liberated futures contract and one would not be wrong in thinking that.

Throughout the section, I have encouraged you to play with the idea of the option and try your best to be creative and imaginative with the idea and I encourage you to continue. In the event, that you are a person who is not flush with cash then not to worry! As long as you have the internet, you can still be creative and play with options. There are various simulators out there, which allow anyone to sign up for free and play around with the markets. However, do note that options are complex securities, therefore, I suggest that you start with simulators that only do stocks and then try your hand at option trading.

The (Actual) Conclusion

This chapter has been truly fascinating for me and hopefully for you too because while conducting the research for the chapter, I came across various things that I was not privy to before. Quite honestly, I did not know about the Greeks or option hedging before I started the research for the chapter. But, once I learned about these things, I made sure I understood the fundamentals or the cores of the various ideas I came across. This book is a testament to the fact that understanding the fundamentals or the core, of any subject can really enhance what you know and understand about the subject. Therefore, it is of paramount importance, that you understand the core of what I am talking about otherwise; your learning will be incomplete.

In the next chapter, we will be taking a look at funds. You may have heard about them, you know, mutual funds, hedge funds, index funds, and fund of funds. The possibilities are endless.

Chapter 5

Funds

Since the invention of the "Chorinator", Julian has become more imaginative and more creative than he ever was. He constantly looks for opportunities where he can excel and furthermore, looks for other products that he can improve upon.

Even though the Chorniator, made money, Julian, like most people, wants even more. He is always looking for ways, in which he can expand his capital and diversify his portfolio. He meets with various financial gurus, that offer him advice on the various ways he can invest his money and Julian has heard most of what the gurus have to say. He knows about options and futures and he knows how the various ways he can mitigate risk by using these instruments but Julian wants to go big. He wants the ability to invest in securities which he otherwise cannot because of either his lack of experience or his lack of capital.

"Maybe, there is some sort of institution that can invest for me?" Julian thinks. He consults his mentor about this issue and finds that, he is exactly correct. There do exist institutions that allow you to gain the scope of the larger market without investing heavily or even having the financial know how, of how to invest.

This sounds like a great idea to Julian. What could be the advantages and the disadvantages to this type of investment vehicle? What kind of variety, do these vehicles/institutions provide? What kind of investment vehicles are there? Are all investment vehicles created equally? What separates one vehicle from another? Does anyone regulate these vehicles? What does it take to invest in these vehicles?

So many questions arise as Julian finds that an idea such as an investment vehicle which pools money exists. This is just fantastic! All Julian has to do now, is learn about these institutions and understand exactly how they work in order to make an informed judgement. To Julian, the possibilities are endless!

5.1 Before the Basics

The possibilities are indeed endless, as we learned from Julian's story. Throughout the story, I tried my best to hint at the aspects of funds and ask various questions that you may have over the course of this chapter.

Understanding funds is not difficult once you understand their purpose and a few fundamentals. Afterwards, the idea of funds and their use will come easily to you.

Throughout the chapter, I would like you to think of ways in which you can pool money together and invest in a plethora of securities without owning them directly. Most importantly, I would like you to think about funds in a collective sense rather than individual sense because that is the nature of funds.

Throughout the chapter, I will use the words "funds", "investment vehicles" and "institutions" interchangeably. Within the context of this chapter, institutions can be referred to as funds but do note that there are various institutions that are not funds, for example, banks or investment banks.

This chapter is unique in some sense because it employs all of the information that you have learned, and hopefully understood, into the topic of funds. Therefore, this chapter will be a great way for you to gauge yourself in your knowledge and understanding. Not only will this chapter cover funds but it will also cover various strategies that the funds apply to which will allow you to see how funds invest and in some ways, the various strategies individuals employ. Thus, I encourage you to pay very close attention in this chapter more than you have in the other chapters.

5.2   The Basics

Throughout the previous two pages, I have been mentioning the phrase "pool money together" or some variant of it and for good reason. Funds are exactly that, they are individuals who have come together to pool money in order to gain a profit.

> Fund: An investment vehicle that is
> made up of a pool of money collected
> from investors. (Investopedia.com)

Presume, you wanted to start investing in various stock and bonds but had relatively low capital. So you meet up with numerous friends who are interested in investing but also have relatively low capital to invest. So, you and your buddies comes up with a genius idea. Why not pool our money together and take a percentage of the profits? That way, even with the low investing capital, we are still able to invest in numerous stocks and bonds. This idea shares exactly the same purpose as any fund that might exist. The primary point of most funds, I say "most" because there funds that are reserved for people with lots of capital is to provide people with, low investing capital, an alternative way to invest in a magnitude of securities.

There are various funds that exist in the markets that provide a wide range of possibilities and provide a broad range of variety. Here is a quick list of some of the funds that exist within the markets.

- Mutual Funds

    – Index Funds

- Fund of funds

- Exchange Traded Funds

- Money Market Funds

- Hedge Funds

These are just to name a few types of funds that exist. As a matter of fact, there exist funds that are geared specifically towards various sectors in the markets. For example, there are funds that only invest in emerging markets or large market cap funds. You can say that there is a fund for everyone!

5.3   Types of Funds

Most of the funds I mentioned above are known as "open ended funds" and with only two types of funds that exist, the other is a "closed end fund". Within these types exist all the other types of funds, as a matter of fact, one could say that there are types within types. By classifying funds, we are easily able to get a perspective on the fund itself. Think of this classification like classifying assets, whereby knowing the type of the fund can easily give us a look into certain characteristics of the funds themselves. Most funds that we hear about are open ended funds. Being an open ended fund involves a lot of characteristics.

Open Ended Fund

To put simply, an open ended fund is a fund that allows anyone to invest in it and furthermore, is not restricted to distributing more stock then it issued initially. For example, suppose you had a fund that started with 1 000 shares. The fund became extremely popular after its inception and evidently, the demand of the stock went up. In order to allow more than 1 000 investors to invest in the company, the fund decides to issue more stock, say around

500, which allows 500 other individuals to invest in the funds' success.

This is the most important aspect to note about an open ended fund. That being, open ended funds are allowed to distribute more stock if need be. This is the main feature that sets it apart from its counterpart, the closed ended fund.

The NAV

Since, the fund is able to distribute stock and not necessarily on the market, the value of the stock is dependent and is proportional to the NAV or the Net Asset Value. The Net Asset Value is calculated by subtracting the assets from the liabilities and dividing by the number of shares that have been issued. This gives the dollar value per share in the company. Suppose, you had a share in a fund, when you redeem the share, the price of the share will be proportional to the NAV. The NAV is usually a good reflection of the current state of the fund. For example, a fund that has a negative NAV indicates that they have more liabilities than assets which, for the most part, is considered bad. However, the NAV should not be the only calculation that is taken into account when analyzing a fund, there are various other factors one has to analyze before a decision can be made.

The shares that are distributed by open ended funds do not need to be distributed through an exchange and as a matter of fact they are not with one exception (Exchange Traded Fund). Therefore, shares of open ended funds have to be distributed through the manager of the fund or through some secondary market that the fund has created. This is only way an open ended fund can distribute stock without being traded on an exchange like an Exchange Traded Fund or a close ended fund.

Close Ended Fund

Close Ended Funds have the ability to have their stock traded on an exchange because that is one of the only ways they can have their stock traded. As mentioned earlier, close ended funds cannot distribute their stock after their inception and cannot have investors redeem their stock. Therefore, all the stock that a close ended fund wants to distribute, they must distribute it during their inception through an IPO and investors who wish to redeem their shares must do it through a secondary market. This is unlike open ended funds because even though some of them are traded on secondary markets, their shares can still be redeemed through the fund itself (this the primary difference between a closed ended fund and an Exchange Traded Fund).

Unlike open ended funds whose shares directly reflect their NAV, that is not the case for close ended funds. Since close ended funds are traded on a secondary market, the price of their stock directly reflects various economic factors. Therefore, you could have a fund that is a value stock and you could have a fund that is a growth stock but that is not typical.

Closed ended funds are generally interested in more specific sectors in an economy. Where an open ended fund may be interested in most if not all aspects of the markets, a close ended fund may only be interested in a specific sector of the market. For example, a close ended fund may only be interested in the energy market or the emerging market sector.

Both open ended and close ended funds have various funds such as mutual funds and hedge funds that operate under either one of them. It is important to say that being a certain fund such as a hedge fund does not mean that that fund directly falls under "close ended fund". There is no correlation between the type of fund and the fund itself. Thus, one cannot assume that all hedge funds, for example, will be close ended.

5.4   Active and Passive Management

Both open ended funds and close ended funds can be managed either actively or passively. More often than not, you will notice on the news that the anchors refer to people known as "fund managers". The name means exactly what you think it means, a person who manages the fund. However, managing a fund can have various meanings depending on whether the fund is managed passively or managed actively.

Active management has more to do with investing rather than tracking. Fund managers that govern various actively managed funds are required to pick stocks or other assets. Active management is used in funds such as hedge funds and money market funds. The main advantage with active management/active investing is that it gives the investor an opportunity to "beat the market", which means to perform better than the market. For example, if a fund has gained 5% and the market has only gained 2% then it can be said that the fund has "beat the market". Of course, with the rewards that come with the opportunity of beating the market, there also come risks. Due to fact that funds employ strategies that passively managed funds do not, an investor can be assured that actively managed funds, some more than others, are riskier than passively managed funds.

Where active management allows the fund manager to pick the stock/asset, passive managements require the fund manager to replicate the market. In other words, a fund such as an index fund is required to track the market and replicate its gains and losses. For example, if the market was up 1% then you would expect an index fund to be up relatively the same amount and if the market is down 1% then we could expect an index fund to be down the same amount.

This is the basis behind passively managed funds. Their primary purpose is to reflect the markets and try not to beat the markets. Therefore, passively managed funds are less risky in general, than actively managed funds but provide less return on investment than actively managed funds.

In the end, both styles of management have their advantage and disadvantages. The debate is primarily between risk and return and this debate is eternal. Some say that passively managed funds are better because they provide more safety but then the rebuttal is that they do not provide a good reward. Likewise, proponents of active management will say that their side provides more reward but here the response is that they are too risky. This debate will continue forever because it is all dependent on the personality of the investor or what the investor requires in their portfolio.

5.5 Securities and Exchange Commission

The SEC is quite prevalent in the news, mostly for controversy, because every now and then people feel that they are regulating less than they should or people feel that they are regulating more than they should. So, one can say they are, in some ways, trapped between a rock and a hard place.

The SEC is a regulatory commission that oversees securities and their creation and their general "well-being", they are also responsible for keeping an eye on various exchanges that operate within their domain, which is the entire United States. But more importantly and more relevant to the topic at hand, they are responsible for overseeing/regulating institutions such as funds.

The SEC requires that all companies that are publicly trading provide financial statements in order for investors to see if they are making the correct decision in the investment. The purpose behind this is to give investors a chance to "stay away from trouble" using the best of their judgement. For example, if John bought company A for $200 without knowing that company A was going to be bankrupt soon and did not have the opportunity to become aware of this then that is not fair to John and other investors like him. Therefore, in order to keep the playing field level, SEC requires publicly trading companies to distribute yearly and quarterly reports about the status of their company.

Since, funds are publicly trading remember that they distribute their stock to the public through a secondary market, they are also required to provide financial statements to their investors. However, funds such as hedge funds are not required by the SEC to provide any sort of financial statements to the public and that is because of the fact that hedge funds do not distribute their stock to the general public or retail investors, investors who trade from their personal account (`Investopedia.com`).

5.6   The Specifics

As mentioned earlier in the chapter, there are various funds that exist, with the most common being the mutual fund. Through this section, I would like to give you the details of the various funds that exist and how they operate.

The Mutual Fund

This is something that we hear all the time "which mutual fund are you invested in?" and that is because they are extremely popular and readily available. The primary purpose of mutual funds is to offer investors an opportunity to invest in various portions of the markets with little investment capital.

Mutual fund is a broad category; as a matter of fact most funds are considered "mutual funds". For example, there exist passively managed funds such as index funds, that we discussed earlier, that are considered mutual funds. In addition, there are common mutual funds that employ active management. Therefore, "mutual fund" is a common name that is used to describe funds that have specific characteristics.

Diversification

Mutual funds are most commonly used by retail investors because of the fact that they provide the investor with experience that the investor may or may not have. They also, provide the investor with something known as diversification, which is a type of investment strategy and is most commonly described through the proverb "Don't put all of your eggs in the same basket."

Suppose, you had a portfolio that consisted of one stock that you believed strongly in. Any gains or losses that occur on the stock, directly reflect the net gain or net loss in your portfolio because, well, you only have one stock and its wins and losses are the portfolio's wins and losses.

However, would it not be more beneficial for you to own two stocks, so just in case one stock does badly, the other can cover for it or at least minimize the damage? You decide now that you will have two stocks within your portfolio in order to reduce the risk. But if stocks are not doing well that year and you would like a steady stream of returns. So you decide the investing in the fixed interest asset class is a good way to mitigate risk because (1), the class is known for its low risk and (2) the class provides steady stream of interest.

This is the central idea behind diversification. The notion that distributing your eggs into numerous baskets will keep a majority of them safe, just in-case one of the baskets breaks. Keeping with the analogy, imagine that you had all your eggs in one basket, then if that basket broke, you would lose all of them and have nothing left. By investing into various different securities you are keeping your money safe. More often than not, retail investors will have their mind set to invest in a few stocks but again "one should not keep all of their eggs in the same basket", therefore, they will try to diversify their portfolio by investing various mutual funds.

The question, now, is how do mutual funds ensure diversification? Due to the large capital they have at hand, they can invest in numerous sectors in the market and effectively, mitigate risk that might occur. For example, if the energy sector is doing well and the emerging markets sector is not then, it is possible that the gain from the energy stocks mitigates the losses gained more the emerging markets. Furthermore, if the fund is actively managed then it can be expected that the fund has an experienced fund manager who knows what he/she is doing. With this in mind, investing in a mutual fund provides a sense of security and experience to the investors' portfolio.

Since mutual funds are available to the general public, they are required to follow certain practices such as daily liquidity. As we talked about earlier, open ended mutual funds allow investors to redeem their shares; daily liquidity gives them the ability to do that at the end of every day and for that matter, any day. Every mutual fund must abide by this, otherwise they are not considered a mutual fund e.g. hedge fund.

It can be seen that mutual funds have government oversight to ensure that the playing field is level. This, again, makes them popular to the general public, which they governed towards anyway.

Mutual funds are a great way for retail investors to diversify their portfolio and also allow them to invest in a wide variety of assets without investing too much of their own capital. It allows investors to add, alongside diversification, experience to their portfolio.

Exchange Traded Fund

While we are on the topic of mutual funds, it's good to give a shout out to the increasingly popular Exchange Traded Fund (ETF), primarily because it acts like an open ended fund and a close ended fund. An ETF, is fund that is traded on an exchange, like the name suggests. This makes the fund much like a close ended fund but let's not stop there. Even though the ETF has shares that are available on an exchange, they also allow the investor to redeem their shares whose price is dependent on the NAV. This makes the ETF like an open ended fund.

ETFs generally tend to track various indexes much like index funds, except index funds are not exchange traded. You may find numerous ETFs that track the same index as an index fund but one of the only things that sets them apart is the fact that ETFs trade on an exchange and index funds do not. In addition to tracking indexes, there are ETFs that are actively managed but this is rare.

Overall, ETFs provide an alternative look into mutual funds because they in some sense, are not the conventional mutual fund but in another sense they are.

Hedge Funds

These are, by far, one of the most mysterious things that exist on Wall Street primarily because they are extremely secretive and they have good reason to be.

Hedge funds or *hedged* funds gained their names because of the strategy used during their early days to invest. Over time, the "d" in hedged got chopped off and now we are left with hedge. You already know the meaning of "hedge", which we described in the previous chapter.

To reiterate, hedging involves the tactic of mitigating risk. This is done through various securities and strategies that are employed by fund managers. The most common hedging strategy is shorting. We talked about a short position but not so much about shorting itself. Shorting involves buying a security on margin and then hoping to sell it back for a profit.

For example, stock ABC is priced at $10 but you believe that it will drop so you borrow this stock and sell it. Assuming you have 100 shares, you make $1000 but you still owe 100 shares to the person you got the shares from. Luckily for you the price of the stock drops to $5, at which point you buy 100 shares for $5 which totals to $500 and you return those shares from the person you owe therefore, you profited $500.

When the price of the security fell, you gained money which is a good thing when you are trying to hedge your portfolio against risk, even though it is not conventional to do it through stocks. When the price of your security falls, it means you gain and if at the same time, the price of another security decreased then you would have mitigated some of the loss because of the short you had in place.

Shorting is used this way by numerous hedge funds but not all.

Types of Hedge Funds

There are numerous types of hedge funds that exist. Their type is generally classified by the strategy that they use. For example, there are hedge funds that are called "global macro hedge funds" because of the global macro strategy that they apply.

I will not go into detail of these strategies because they vary from fund to fund and furthermore, are beyond the scope of this book to describe. As a matter of fact, there are entire books that are only published on type one of investment style.

The global macro strategy involves analysing various macro economic trends such as interest rates, GDP and on the basis of their analysis they invest in various markets. The largest hedge fund in the world by assets under management, Bridgewater Associates, is a global macro hedge fund.

There are also funds known as quantitative funds and the people that work at these funds are known as "quants". Quants seek to apply various algorithms and statistical models to do their analysis on the markets. Where global macro deals with the larger part of the market, quantitative funds try to find a part in the market which they can exploit.

The reason why these funds are so secretive is because of the strategies that they employ and the information that they have. In essence, if everyone is a millionaire then no-one is a millionaire or, in other words, if everyone exploits a weak point in the market then that point becomes like any other point and thus, there is nothing special about the point.

I have only mentioned two types of hedge funds but there are numerous types such as market neutral funds or event driven funds.

What makes a Hedge Fund different?

Aside from the various strategies and the secrecy that is implemented, hedge funds employ interesting performance fees and are unable to market themselves among other things. Hedge funds are not for retail investors and as a matter of fact, a large amount of capital, generally higher than one million dollars, is required to invest in one. Due to this, hedge funds are not regulated by the SEC heavily. But with the perk of not being regulated, hedge funds are not allowed to advertise themselves. All of the advertisements are done through word-of-mouth.

Unlike mutual funds that provide daily liquidity, hedge funds provide liquidity every six months or sometimes every year. It is extremely difficult to implement complex strategies when there is a possibility that investors might pull their cash, in a slight down turn. Hedge funds require that investors in their fund have "faith" and not withdraw capital as soon as a little red is shown. Aside from this, hedge funds also employ what is known as the "two and twenty". The two and twenty is the performance fee and management fee, respectively, that managers take in return for letting you invest money into their fund.

The Two and Twenty   The two and twenty works likes so. Suppose, you had $5 million and you chose to invest it into a hedge fund that employed the two and twenty. Then you would be subject to paying a 2% management fee and a 20% performance fee. If, your investment of $5 million grew by 10% then 20% of the 10% which is 2% would be given to the hedge fund managers and you would have 8% as your gain. The management fee is found by finding 2% of the NAV.

This two and twenty has been slightly controversial but has sustained itself within the industry over time. However, it is not necessary that all funds implement the two and twenty. Furthermore, some funds are known to implement a one and twenty but that is not common.

Everyone wants Alpha

Hedge fund managers and hedge funds have an obsession with the term "alpha", everyone is chasing alpha. Alpha, basically, is the value that states how much the fund has beaten its benchmark by. Alpha can also be seen as the absolute returns of a fund.

Technically, alpha is the volatility of a fund and compares its risk adjusted performance to a benchmark. For example, a fund that has an alpha of 10 is said to have beaten its benchmark by 10%. Hedge funds strive for alpha because they are expected to have it. Regardless of the state of the market, down or up, they are expected to beat it every single time and as a matter of fact, there are funds that have been beating the market every year for the past 20 years!

Wrapping Up

Mutual funds are a great opportunity for investors to pool money in order to invest in various securities that they otherwise could not afford. With the variety that is provided, the possibilities are endless.

Over the chapter, we discussed various strategies that funds employ in order to beat the market or to have a better portfolio. Even though it may be extremely difficult to think of a strategy and implement it, I encourage you to seek new ways and develop new ideas to beat the markets yourself. It is not necessary that you develop new ideas but it can be extremely useful to improve existing ideas. The purpose is not to actually make a new strategy or improve another, it is to get yourself thinking of the markets in a broader scope and to allow your imagination and creativity to flourish.

Looking Back

It Has Been An Adventure

This book started off as a way to get less sleep but eventually led to something more than that. Aside from reducing the amount of sleep I got, the purpose was to learn and to learn well. To understand the fundamentals of any subject is profound because it appeals to persons' logos more than anything.

When I was researching for this book, I realized that the markets were more than what people though they were. More often than not, I come across individuals who think that the markets are only a bunch of numbers and nothing more. They require no creativity and no imagination whatsoever but I have to say that notion is extremely erroneous. Finance requires just as much creativity as Art or Mathematics or Physics but the way in which it is expressed is much different. Throughout the book, examples were provided to jog your creativity and imagination and I continue to encourage you to do that. Ideas are required in any field before numbers and this includes finance, therefore, continue to be imaginative and creative. Don't be afraid to be wrong in your imagination because that is one of the only ways you will be able to develop newer ideas. Constantly, I find that individuals are afraid of being wrong, I don't know why but they are, don't be afraid to be wrong because I guarantee you will not be able to learn to your fullest extent.

The Fundamentals

While writing this book, I realized that the key to learning was to learn the fundamentals. The fundamentals involved learning exactly how the topic worked and what were its foundations.

At the beginning of the book, I introduced the idea of building a strong foundation and at the end, I still am stressing this fact. Building a strong foundation is extremely important because they recur whenever you are learning a new topic. In the field of finance it is extremely important that you have the ability to make inferences well and without having strong fundamentals and foundations, it is extremely difficult to make inferences as well as someone who has strong fundamentals and foundations.

This is Not the End

Even though the book is complete and you have learned what the book has to offer do not stop! The field is extremely vast and it has fields within fields. Pick one chapter within the book and learn more than the basics. You will see that one idea can lead to another which will lead to another and this process will expand your horizon more than you think. The most important thing I can recommend is that you absorb financial materials as much as possible because this will build on what you know and furthermore, permit you to apply what you know.

It is one thing to know but it another to apply and therefore, I recommend that you do both daily. It was the purpose of this book to have informed readers by the end and I hope I have achieved that goal.

ABOUT THE AUTHOR

Jeel Shah is a grade 12 high school student who loves to learn new things and explore the world for what it is. His interest for economics and the markets was first piqued in grade 8 and from then on, it has only been a journey. His other interests lie in physics, computer science and philosophy.

P.S. That isn't my bird.